OXFORD STUDIES IN THEOLOGICAL ETHICS

General Editor: Oliver O'Donovan

OXFORD STUDIES IN THEOLOGICAL ETHICS

The series presents discussions on topics of general concern to Christian Ethics, as it is currently taught in universities and colleges, at the level demanded by a serious student. The volumes will not be specialized monographs nor general introductions or surveys. They aim to make a contribution worthy of notice in its own right but also focused in such a way as to provide a suitable starting-point for orientation.

The titles include studies in important contributors to the Christian tradition of moral thought; explorations of current moral and social questions; and discussions of central concepts in Christian moral and political thought. Authors treat their topics in a way that will show the relevance of the Christian tradition, but with openness to neighbouring traditions of thought which have entered into dialogue with it.

Double-Effect Reasoning

Doing Good and Avoiding Evil

T. A. CAVANAUGH

CLARENDON PRESS · OXFORD

OXFORD

UNIVERSITY PRESS

Great Clarendon Street, Oxford OX2 6DP

Oxford University Press is a department of the University of Oxford.
It furthers the University's objective of excellence in research, scholarship,
and education by publishing worldwide in

Oxford New York

Auckland Cape Town Dar es Salaam Hong Kong Karachi
Kuala Lumpur Madrid Melbourne Mexico City Nairobi
New Delhi Shanghai Taipei Toronto

With offices in

Argentina Austria Brazil Chile Czech Republic France Greece
Guatemala Hungary Italy Japan Poland Portugal Singapore
South Korea Switzerland Thailand Turkey Ukraine Vietnam

Oxford is a registered trade mark of Oxford University Press
in the UK and in certain other countries

Published in the United States
by Oxford University Press Inc., New York

British Library Cataloguing in Publication Data

Data available

Library of Congress Cataloguing in Publication Data

Data available

Typeset by SPI Publisher Services, Pondicherry, India
Printed in Great Britain
on acid-free paper by
Biddles Ltd., King's Lynn

ISBN 978-0-19-927219-8

Acknowledgements

Reading Alan Donagan's critique, I came upon double effect, which has interested me for the past decade. That interest culminates in this book. In my graduate work at the University of Notre Dame, Professor David Solomon introduced me to double effect while Professor Ralph McInerny directed and supported my work. I thank them. Over the years, I discussed double effect with many colleagues and students. I thank Professors Joe Boyle, Kevin Flannery, Jorge Garcia, John Haldane, Christopher Kaczor, Edward Lyons, Stephen McPhee, Don Marquis, and my University of San Francisco colleagues, particularly Professors Raymond Dennehy and Michael Torre. Of the many students at the University of San Francisco with whom I have been privileged to philosophize, I particularly thank Mr Logan Sims (who scrupulously checked references) and those in my double-effect seminar. I thank the audiences to whom I have spoken, in particular those at Marquette, Notre Dame, Saint Mary's College of California, Stanford, and, my alma mater, Thomas Aquinas College, whose tutors, in particular Ronald McArthur and Thomas Dillon, have encouraged me over the years.

I owe Reverend Oliver O'Donovan a large debt of gratitude for eliminating imprecisions and infelicities from the present work, while retaining faith in the same. I also thank Ms Lucy Qureshi and Mr Jeff New for their thoughtful assistance with the manuscript and typescript. I lay claim to any and all remaining errors.

This work represents myriad re-visions of how to think about double effect. Earlier approaches appeared elsewhere. Small portions of what I consider best in those attempts here survive. I acknowledge and thank *The Thomist* for that portion of Chapter 1, the *Aquinas Review* for that of Chapter 2, and the *American Catholic Philosophical Quarterly, Cambridge Quarterly of Healthcare Ethics, Christian Bioethics, Journal of Applied Philosophy,* and

Philosophical Papers for those portions of Chapters 3, 4, and 5 that appeared earlier.

I thank the Mortimer Fleishhacker Endowment for Philosophy at the University of San Francisco for financial support which enabled me to devote a sabbatical to completing this work. Finally, for their patience with and sustained interest in casuistry, I thank those to whom I dedicate this work: my wife and son.

T. A. Cavanaugh

San Francisco
January 2006

Dedication
To Bonnie, for being so; to Thomas, for calling to find out more.

Contents

Introduction

Do good. Avoid evil. Taken generally, these foundational moral norms offer us clear guidance. The good has the nature of what we ought to pursue; evil, what we should flee. We should preserve ourselves and avoid destruction. We ought to reproduce and rear our offspring while warding off the harms a sharp-edged world poses. We ought to seek knowledge and live with others while shunning ignorance and eschewing offence to our neighbours. Eating, drinking, clothing, sheltering, copulating, teaching, and talking instance acts seeking good and avoiding evil.

Yet, as we pursue good and avoid evil, a tangled mass confronts us. The good we do results in evil; the evil we avoid prevents the realization of some good. The oncologist who seeks to cure by chemotherapy also nauseates, debilitates, and sickens his patient. The mother who admonishes her daughter also embarrasses her before peers. The maker of a legitimate product—a drug, spray paint, or glue—finds that others abuse it. One need not multiply examples. These quotidian experiences and a moment's reflection indicate that the good one should seek and the evil one ought to avoid inextricably bind at times. In such circumstances how ought we to act? If one were to pursue the good, one would cause the very evil one ought to avoid. Yet, if one were to avoid the associated evils, one would not achieve the goods of health, discipline, merited praise, and so on. In such circumstances, can one do good and avoid evil? If so, how?

To engage the most serious cases in terms of which thinkers have addressed these questions, consider the following scenarios. Your terminally ill patient experiences severe pain. In order to relieve her otherwise intractable pain you must sedate her with barbiturates that will also suppress her respiration. Relieved of pain, she will be asphyxiated and die.[1] In another situation, your terminally ill patient suffers severe pain. She thinks that she would be better off dead; she repeatedly requests a lethal injection.

You can destroy the enemy artillery installation by tactical bombing. However, given the proximity of the artillery to the hospital and the imprecision and destructive force of your bombs, you know that if you bomb you will kill and maim the patients in the hospital. In another case, your commander proposes to lower the enemy's morale by terror bombing the hospital.[2]

---

[1] I call this terminal sedation. For a description of an actual instance, see e.g. the case Ira Byock, MD, a hospice physician expert in palliation, presents (Byock 1997, 209–16). Fortunately, one typically need not resort to terminal sedation to relieve pain at the end of life. As Byock notes, however, there remain instances in which one can relieve pain only by sedation.

[2] Some refer to what I call tactical bombing as strategic bombing. 'Strategic' is especially unsuitable; during World War II the primary responsibility of the Royal Air Force's Office of Strategic Bombing was the terror bombing of non-combatants.

Pregnant, you have just been informed that you also have life-threatening uterine cancer. Your doctor must remove the cancerous uterus before the foetus is viable. If you have the hysterectomy necessary to preserve your life, the foetus will die. In another case, you are in labour, but the baby's head is too large to exit the birth canal. Nothing can be done for both of you. The doctor can save your life by decapitating the baby; or do nothing, and you both die, you die and the child lives, or the child dies and you live.[3]

A torpedo strikes the bow of a submarine and explodes. Water floods the forward compartments. The submarine begins to sink. The captain commands you to close the flood-door. You will thereby trap the submariners at the bow in a watery grave. Yet, if the door remains open, you, the entire crew, and the submarine itself will be lost. In a different scenario, the submarine has sunk. Fortunately, you and your fellow crew members escaped. You find yourself marooned; food has run out. In order to feed the crew, the captain commands you to kill just as many submariners as would have been killed by closing the watertight door. If you do not, the entire crew will starve.

---

[3] One calls this procedure an obstetric craniotomy. The procedure addresses rarely occurring cephalo-pelvic disproportion in which the child's head (cephalo) is too large to exit from the mother's birth canal (pelvic). 'Craniotomy' denotes the cutting of the cranium. As used in the present work, the term refers to an obstetric craniotomy. In an obstetric craniotomy, a physician cuts a hole in the baby's head, removes its brain, and dismembers its skull. Fortunately, the (already small) number of such grisly cases has almost been eliminated in developed countries, due to better prenatal care that discovers disproportion and prepares for delivery via Caesarian section. (For a detailed description of an obstetric craniotomy, see Williams 1985, 1140–2).

One errs in thinking that ethics primarily concerns such conflicted life-and-death situations. More generally, one goes awry in holding that circumstances in which good inextricably binds with evil preoccupy ethics. Nonetheless, responses to such cases answer the questions this work addresses; namely, whether and how one can do good and avoid evil in circumstances inseparably joining the two. Moreover, how one addresses these cases sheds light on the earlier-noted ordinary instances of acting when good binds with bad. For example, does the oncologist act well entirely because the good of curing outweighs the bad of temporarily sickening, or must one take into account other factors, such as his intent? Would the overall goodness of the mother's act of disciplining her daughter be diminished or even vitiated if she also sought to embarrass?

One straightforward solution to hard cases calculates the goods and evils in each scenario. Comparing these—counting the dead and living—and giving weight solely to such consequentialist considerations leads one in the last pair of cases, for example, to close the doors and to kill the submariners for food. In a consequentialist ethic all choices (including hard ones) have essentially the same solution: opt for that scenario having the greatest net good consequences or the least net bad consequences. In such an ethic, innocence has ethical import, but only up to a point. The relative amounts of good and bad alone decisively matter. (Moreover, as we shall see in section 4.2, a consequentialist ethic does not acknowledge the import of intent in the evaluation of acts.)

For an ethic incorporating exceptionless moral norms such cases pose serious difficulties. In this work, I assume that there are exceptionless moral norms; particularly that it is always wrong intentionally to take the life of or grievously harm the innocent.[4] Before addressing whether and how one can do good and avoid evil in circumstances inextricably binding the two and implicating the norm against killing the innocent, the latter requires articulation. To what does the acceptance of this norm commit one?

'Innocent' admits of ambiguity; literally, it means not harmful. One innocent in the literal sense does not physically pose a threat. Call him materially innocent. A person possessing material innocence enjoys inviolability under the norm. What of those lacking material innocence (namely, those who pose a threat)? Refer to them as materially responsible.[5] Amongst the materially responsible, some pose the threat with knowledge and control (with voluntariness) while others do so without knowledge or control (without voluntariness). Consider the former group first. Call them formally responsible. For example, consider a police officer and his assailant both of whom point a gun at one another. Both have material responsibility for threatening one an-

[4] I understand the norm against killing the innocent to prohibit the intent to kill or grievously harm the innocent. Including grievous harm in the norm both agrees with the common-sense interpretation of why one ought not to kill the innocent (because killing profoundly harms) and represents the long-standing legal and moral interpretations of what the norm against killing prohibits. The norm against killing the innocent prohibits killing, maiming, putting into persistent vegetative states, paralyzing, and so on.

[5] At this stage, one avoids 'guilt' insofar as it connotes wrongness (lack of a justification). Prior to examining the justification (or lack thereof) for the posing of the threat, one focuses on to whom one may attribute the threat.

other. Moreover, both do so with knowledge and control. Therefore, in addition to material responsibility, they both have formal responsibility. In order to determine who enjoys inviolability under the norm, one asks: does either have a justification for posing the threat? If the assailant threatens the officer insofar as the officer prevents him from taking another's property, the officer possesses while the assailant lacks a justification. The officer retains innocence while the assailant does not. The norm protects the officer but not the assailant (bearing in mind caveats concerning the use of non-lethal force, proportionateness, and so on). Of course, were the assailant to stop threatening the officer, he, too, would enjoy inviolability under the norm.

Now consider the latter group of the materially responsible; namely, those who pose the threat without knowledge or control (without voluntariness). Refer to this group as innocent threats. An innocent threat lacks material innocence insofar as he poses a threat (has material responsibility). Yet, he possesses what one may refer to as formal innocence. Lack of beliefs, desires, intent, in short, the absence of voluntariness respecting one's being harmful constitutes formal innocence.[6] An innocent threat threatens without voluntariness. (Imagine a person infected with a highly contagious lethal disease, who, through no fault of his own, poses a lethal threat to others.)

---

[6] Within criminal law, the principle, *actus non facit reum, nisi mens sit rea* captures the point at issue. The bad doing of posing a threat (*actus*) does not make the crime (*reum*), absent the mental element (*mens rea*). For a related discussion, see sec. 2.2.1.

Does the norm against killing the innocent extend to innocent threats? Some think that one may justifiably kill an innocent threat (see, for example, Alan Donagan's account in section 2.2.1). If this were so, the exceptionless norm at issue would amount to something like, 'killing or severely injuring the materially innocent (physically harmless) and those amongst the formally responsible who possess a justification is never justifiable'.[7] In this work, I understand innocence as including, but not being limited to, material innocence. That is, the norm at issue states, 'it is always seriously wrong to kill or grievously harm the materially innocent, the formally responsible who possess a justification for posing a threat, and the formally innocent'. That is, one always does a serious wrong when one kills or grievously harms a person who does not threaten at all, threatens with a justification, or does not voluntarily threaten.[8] This norm appears more reasonable than one that would not protect innocent threats. For humans differ most markedly from other beings insofar as they are rational beings who, thereby, act voluntarily. One appropriately relates to another human when one attends to the presence or absence of voluntariness in his conduct. Accordingly,

---

[7] One consequence of this might be that performing the craniotomy would no longer violate the norm. Although, if the child innocently threatens the mother's life so also the mother innocently threatens the child's life. Changing the norm may not entirely resolve the problem. For one then must determine (by a standard other than innocence) both whom to kill and whom to defend.

[8] By 'person' I mean a member of the species *homo sapiens*. Of course, one threatened by a formally innocent person may not know that the innocent threat is innocent. The point is that when one does know, one cannot ethically kill the innocent threat.

formal innocence has ethical significance for inviolability. In any case, I do not argue for this norm; rather, having here articulated it, I assume it.

Many questions attend this norm, most of which I put aside. For example, I do not address the retrospective import of this norm, as it bears on punishing those who violate it. Does capital punishment undermine or vindicate the norm? Moreover, what, precisely, is it to possess a justification while one voluntarily poses a lethal threat? In the example above, I assert that the police officer possesses a justification while his assailant lacks one. As will become evident throughout this work in my consideration of killing in war, I hold that soldiers in a just war possess justifications in their killing of enemy combatants. Again, I note these important matters only to put them aside. Rather, I address the questions of whether and how one can do good and avoid evil when good and evil inextricably bind by considering the most pointed instances of the same, namely, those in which human lives stand in the balance. I answer these questions by considering instances of homicide for a number of reasons. First, in doing so I follow a venerable tradition and the contemporary debate both of which address these questions by considering instances of homicide. Second, such cases simply have perennial interest. Third, and finally, the preservation or loss of a human life instances profound good or evil. Accordingly, it makes sense to address the questions above in terms of human life and death, as many others have done and no doubt will continue to do. I now turn to that task.

The noted cases pose problems to one who holds that killing or seriously harming the innocent is always wrong. For example, does he who closes the submarine's flood-door violate the norm against killing the innocent? A proponent of this norm might say that closing the door is unjust killing, and, therefore, must not be done. Yet, by not closing the flood-door does one not thereby fail to avoid the evil of the remaining crew drowning? Can one do good and avoid evil while accepting the exceptionless wrongness of killing the innocent?

One approach open to one who accepts the norm while not thinking that closing the floor-door need violate it depends upon fundamental concepts that conceptually precede moral evaluation. As G. E. Moore notes, 'ethics is undoubtedly concerned with the question what good conduct is; but, being concerned with this, it obviously does not start at the beginning, unless it is prepared to tell us what is good as well as what is conduct' (Moore 1954, 2). Prior to ethics, one studies what makes conduct conduct. Moral psychology (also referred to as action theory) investigates what makes an action an action by focusing on its mental elements. These elements include knowledge, belief, desire, will, intent, ends, and means. Relying on moral psychology, one asks: 'what conduct, precisely, constitutes unjust killing?' One salient feature of acts this approach attends to is the intention of the agent. It distinguishes between intending to kill or gravely harm, and doing something that has as one of its results the death of or grievous harm to the innocent foreseen as inevitable, but not intended. One distinguishes the intended from the foreseen, even when what

is foreseen is foreseen as inevitable. Employing this distinction (henceforth, the intended/foreseen, or i/f distinction),
closing the flood-door need not violate the norm. Nonetheless, foreseeing that the deaths of the innocent will result
from a course of action militates against pursuing that
action. Thus, in addition to the i/f distinction this response
requires that the agent has some good reason for doing what
will certainly result in the deaths of innocents. This account
of the submarine case and associated cases I call double-
effect reasoning, or DER.[9]

To suggest the continuity of a focus upon intentions in
the evaluation of double-effect cases with our more ordinary
judgements of actions, consider a novel such as Jane
Austen's *Emma*. When the book's eponymous heroine learns
that her protégée Harriet Smith hopes for a marriage
proposal from Mr Knightley, Emma realizes that she herself
loves Knightley. He must marry no one but Emma. Com-
posing herself, she enquires into her friend's evidence for the
improbable match (given their social and temperamental
disparities) of Harriet and Mr Knightley. Miss Smith
recounts the various occasions indicating Mr Knightley's
affections for her, some of which Emma herself witnessed.
Realizing with dread the plausibility of Harriet's interpret-

---

[9] I use the term double-effect reasoning (DER) to refer to what has been
called, variously, the Principle of Double Effect (PDE, Selling 1980), the
Doctrine of Double Effect (DDE, Quinn 1989), and the Rule of Double
Effect (RDE, Ramsey 1978). There are a number of reasons to do so. First,
it is not a principle, but, principally, a set of criteria. Second, thinkers often
reduce it to one criterion, and 'principle' reinforces this erroneous reduction.
'Doctrine' denotes an authoritative teaching, while DER stands on firm
philosophical ground.

ation of Knightley's behaviour, Emma exerts herself to say: 'Harriet, I will only venture to declare, that Mr. Knightley is the last man in the world, who would intentionally give any woman the idea of his feeling for her more than he really does' (Austen 1991, III. xi. 421). Emma implicitly and favourably compares Knightley to Frank Churchill, who does intentionally give false impressions. In fact, Knightley does not love Harriet; nor does he seek to deceive her into thinking he does. Rather, he acts honestly (in attempting to match Harriet with her earlier rebuffed suitor, Mr Martin); Emma and Harriet misunderstand him. They mistake him, however, only up to a point. For Emma correctly notes that Knightley would never intentionally deceive. This remains a fixed point in her interpretation of his conduct. Because of this unchanging truth about his behaviour (and his caution not to reveal his actual intent to Emma, who had mischievously prevented the match of Harriet and Mr Martin), this impossible match of Harriet and George Knightley is, 'far, very far, from impossible,' from Emma's perspective (ibid., III. xi. 423). The importance of intent in understanding and evaluating conduct plays a large role in this novel, as in other works by Austen and other keen observers of daily human intercourse. Of course, she does not address how one evaluates acts when good inextricably binds with evil. Nevertheless, her presentation of the role of intent in the ordinary commerce of life suggests what one might attend to in considering such cases. Moreover, one's analysis of acts in which good binds with evil has plausibility partially to the extent to which it agrees with our day-to-day evaluations of day-to-day acts as exemplified in a writer such as Austen. With this in mind, let us return to our subject.

Typically, exceptionless moral norms serve as the point of departure for double-effect reasoning. Accordingly, it would be mistaken to argue that double effect does not establish the serious wrongness of, for example, killing or grievously harming the innocent. For one's commitment to the norm leads one to employ double-effect reasoning. Nevertheless, if one who acknowledges such norms must have recourse to DER in order to resolve hard cases, then to the extent to which such reasoning succeeds or fails, it discloses such norms as tenable or untenable.

Not all who propose double effect do so because of a commitment to exceptionless norms. Some deontologists who do not hold exceptionless moral norms have proposed double effect as differentiating, for example, tactical and terror bombing as more and less justifiable. Thus, DER may resolve hard cases for those who acknowledge exceptionless norms and for those who take a middle path between consequentialism on the one hand and an ethics including such norms on the other.[10] All proponents of DER

[10] Among such non-absolutist anti-consequentialist thinkers are Foot (1985), Nagel (1986), Quinn (1989), and Sterba (1992). Boyle and Donagan separately argue that non-absolutist anti-consequentialists superfluously employ double effect (Boyle 1991; Donagan 1977, 156–63). I do not argue against those who do not acknowledge exceptionless moral norms and use double-effect reasoning. I argue for the tenability of double-effect reasoning, assuming the exceptionless moral norm against killing or grievously harming the innocent. Again, I do not argue for the norm except to the extent to which arguments for double effect partially defend the tenability of such a norm. Insofar as DER resolves hard cases generated by such norms, successfully to argue for DER establishes the reasonableness of such norms.

reject consequentialism's founding claim; namely, that in evaluating an act consequences *alone* matter. Given this consequentialist commitment, the i/f distinction cannot have moral relevance in act-evaluation. For intent and foresight can result in otherwise similar consequences (as stipulated in the debate and as is indeed sometimes the case). Thus, DER represents one of the principal conflicted points regarding consequentialism's foundation. Accordingly, while some dispute the ethical import of DER, none doubt the more general importance of the controversy for overarching ethical accounts.

In this work, I assume the exceptionless and serious wrongness of intentionally killing or grievously harming the innocent.[11] I focus on consequentially comparable cases involving killing or gravely harming the innocent. I consider three pairs of classically contrasted cases: terminal sedation/euthanasia; tactical bombing/terror bombing; and hysterectomy/craniotomy. I argue that one may justify the first member of each pair in accordance with DER while holding that the second member cannot be justified.

In the first chapter I present the historical background of DER, beginning with Aquinas's account of a private individual's homicidal self-defence and concluding with a consideration of the Jesuit theologian J. P. Gury's nineteenth-century formulation of the criteria of double effect. In the

---

[11] Being wrong without exception and being gravely wrong often coincide. One would err, however, if one were to think that to break an exceptionless norm would be, thereby, to do grave wrong. For example, Augustine and Aquinas argue that lying is exceptionlessly wrong while holding that many lies are peccadillos. For Aquinas's discussion, see *Summa theologiae*, II–II q. 110.

second chapter I consider contemporary offshoots, such as proportionalism; alternatives, such as Alan Donagan's casuistry of material guilt and Frances Kamm's non-absolutist Principle of Permissible Harm; and recent presentations of double effect, such as that of Warren Quinn and the trio of Finnis, Grisez, and Boyle. I devote the third and fourth chapters to considering the i/f distinction. I do so in Chapter 3 by presenting the resources in terms of which one distinguishes intent from foresight. In Chapter 4 I attend to the more controversial issue of the ethical relevance of this distinction, finding its import both in broadly Aristotelian-Thomistic features of action as voluntary and in a Kantian focus on the victim as an end in himself. I conclude the work in Chapter 5 by considering DER's application to allowings and to the wrongful acts of other agents as they depend upon one's own otherwise good act. Moreover, I indicate how international laws bearing on the conduct of war, the laws and public policies of individual countries, constitutional legal systems that incorporate exceptionless legal norms, and the official moral dogmas of the Roman Catholic Church employ DER.

1

The history of double-effect reasoning

1.1. AQUINAS'S ORIGINATING ACCOUNT

Historians of philosophy often attribute DER *tout court* to the medieval theologian-cum-philosopher St Thomas Aquinas (*c*.1225–74) in his consideration of homicidal self-defence.[1] As will become evident upon closer examination, however, Thomas considers the ethical status of risking an assailant's life (*Summa theologiae* II-II q.64 a.7) while contemporary accounts focus on actions causing harm foreseen as inevitable.[2] Moreover, double effect plays a very small role

---

[1] The standard article on the history of DER—and its origin in Aquinas—is Mangan (1949). One does well also to read Ghoos (1951). As will become evident, Ghoos differs from Mangan as to precisely where one finds double effect in Aquinas and to whom one should primarily attribute its development after Aquinas. More recently, Rojas (1995) nicely indicates the historical precedents to Aquinas's account. I rely on all three.

[2] Unless otherwise noted, citations of Aquinas refer to his *Summa theologiae*, translations by the author. In the reference II-II q.64 a.7 obj. 1 s.c. c ad 1, 'II-II' refers to the second part of the second part of the tripartite *Summa*, 'q.' refers to the question, 'a.' to the article, 'obj.' to the objection, 's.c.' to the *sed contra* (i.e. the respected opinion that opposes the preceding objections), 'c' to the corpus of the article (representing Aquinas's considered position), and 'ad' to his response to the objection.

in Aquinas's massive *oeuvre*. He relies on it most explicitly in his consideration of a private individual's homicidal self-defence. One also discerns double-effect reasoning in his consideration of scandal (II-II q.43 a.1 ad 4) and of permissible alluring dress (II-II q.169 a.2).[3] One strains to find him employing it as a general approach to difficult moral cases, however. In sum, Aquinas holds an inchoate form of double effect in a minuscule portion of his work. Nonetheless, a thorough treatment of double effect calls for a consideration of Aquinas's originating version. After considering Thomas's account and his reliance upon his predecessors, I trace the development of double effect through St Antoninus (1389–1459), Cajetan (1469–1534), Vitoria (*c.*1492–1546), Suarez (1548–1617), John of St Thomas (1589–1644), Domingo de Sta Teresa (1600–1654), John de Lugo (1583–1660), St Alphonsus Liguori (1696–1787), up to the nineteenth-century Jesuit manualist Gury (1801–66), who standardizes double effect into its contemporary form.[4]

Aquinas's discussion of homicidal self-defence found in II-II q.64 a.7 serves as the *locus classicus* of DER. In this question, Aquinas considers the greatest injury to one's neighbour: his death. In article 7, Thomas asks whether it

[3] For example, St Antoninus, the fifteenth-century Dominican archbishop of Florence, understands Aquinas to rely on the import of intent and double-effect criteria in discussion of a woman's ornamentation that allures men (Antoninus 1959, vol. ii, c. 595). Although Thomas does not do so explicitly in the text to which Antoninus refers (II-II q.169 a.2), one reasonably interprets him along these lines.

[4] For a detailed history of casuistry, see Jonsen and Toulmin (1988). For a book-length consideration of the modern history of DER see Ugorji (1985). For differing interpretations of Aquinas's account, see Boyle (1978), Cavanaugh (1997), Matthews (1999), and Sullivan (2000).

is licit to kill a man in self-defence. He has earlier argued (II-II q.64 a.2 and a.3), following Augustine, that those charged with the public good, such as a soldier fighting enemy combatants, or a police officer, may take life when doing so serves the common good. Accordingly, in II-II q.64 a.7 Aquinas addresses the morality of a private individual taking the life of an assailant in self-defence. He quotes Augustine, who asks (in *De libero arbitrio* or *On Free Will*), 'how are they free from sin in the sight of divine providence who, for the sake of these contemnible things (*pro his rebus quas contemni*) have taken a human life?' (II-II q.64 a.7 obj.2). Aquinas notes that Augustine includes one's own life among the slight goods that men ought to forfeit rather than kill another. Thus, it appears that a private individual may not take an assailant's life in self-defence. Thomas argues, however, that sometimes a private individual's homicidal self-defence may be justified. He says:

Nothing prevents one act from having two effects, of which only one is intended, the other being *praeter intentionem*. Now moral acts receive their character according to that which is intended, not, however, from that which is *praeter intentionem*, since this is accidental, as is evident from what has been said earlier [II-II q.43 a.3 c]. Thus, from the act of self-defence, two effects may follow: one, the conservation of one's own life; the other, the death of the aggressor. Since what is intended is the conservation of one's own life, such an act is not illicit: it is natural for each thing to preserve itself in existence for as long as it is able. Nevertheless, some act proceeding from a good intention may be rendered illicit if it is not proportioned to the end. Thus, it would not be licit if someone defending his own life were to use more force than necessary.

But, if he repels force with moderation, his defensive act will be licit: for, according to the jurists, 'it is licit to repel force by force, with the moderation of a blameless defence'.[5] Nor is it necessary for salvation that a man forgo an act of moderate force in order to avoid the death of another: since one is more responsible to care for one's own life than someone else's. But, since to kill a man is not licit except for the public authority acting for the sake of the common good (as is evident from what was previously said [II-II q.64 a.3 c]), it is not licit for a man to intend to kill (*intendat occidere*) in order to defend himself, except for those who have public authority. These, intending to kill a man in self-defence, refer this to the public good. This is evident in the case of a soldier fighting an enemy, and in the case of a minister of the judge fighting against thieves. Nevertheless, even these would sin if they were moved by private animosity. (II-II q.64 a.7 c)

Aquinas holds that a private individual may not intentionally kill an aggressor while he may intend self-defence from which the assailant's death results *praeter intentionem*. Aquinas places great emphasis upon the agent's intent. In doing so, he understands himself to be following Augustine, who serves as an authority for Thomas and his audience. Thus, in response to the first objection he asserts that by the phrase, 'for these things', Augustine means to exclude the

[5] Aquinas here quotes the Decretals of Pope Gregory IX, compiled between 1230 and 1234 by Thomas's fellow Dominican St Raymond of Peñafort. The quote (that force may be repelled by force) can be traced back from Pope Innocent III in 1209, through the late Roman jurist Ulpian (*c.*217), to the classical Roman jurist Caius Cassius Longinus (fl. mid-first century AD) In AD 65 Nero banished Caius to Sardinia for showing too great a reverence for his ancestor of the same name, the chief conspirator against Julius Caesar. Ulpian notes that Cassius also holds that one may repel arms by arms.

intentional killing of an assailant. The phrase *pro his rebus* certainly admits of Aquinas's interpretation.

Aquinas did not need to engage in interpretation to discern a focus on intent, however, when he read the accounts of justified homicide found in two of his predecessors, Alan of Lille (*c*.1128–*c*.1202) and Alexander of Hales (*c*.1185–1245). In Alan's *De Fide Catholica* (written between 1185 and 1200), one finds him insisting, as Aquinas will later, that a private individual may repel force with force that results in the death of the aggressor, as long as one is not intending to kill him (*non intendendo eum occidere*) (Alan of Lille 1855, cols. 397–8). Thus, Alan excludes an intent to kill. In contrast to Alan, Alexander of Hales does not focus on the absence of an intent to kill. Rather, in his treatment of the question (found in his *Summa theologica*, the structure of which Aquinas follows closely in his own *Summa theologiae*) he requires that there be an intent to conserve one's own well-being (*intentio conservationis propriae salutis*) (Alexander of Hales 1948, 533). Considering the accounts of Alan and Alexander, one sees an instance of Aquinas's ability to synthesize the thought of those who preceded him and, thereby, to advance the discussion. For in his account he follows Alan in prohibiting an intent to kill and Alexander in requiring an intent to preserve one's own life. In his predecessors' works, one sees the resources upon which Aquinas relies in discussing two effects, one of which the agent intends, the other of which is not intended or is, in Aquinas's terms, *praeter intentionem*.[6]

---

[6] Alonso (1937) and Rojas (1995) illuminate the precedents Aquinas relies on in his discussion of double effect.

What does Thomas mean by *praeter intentionem*? In his use of *praeter intentionem* Aquinas refers his reader to an earlier article, where he maintains that, 'active scandal is accidental when it is *praeter intentionem* of the agent: as when a man by his inordinate deed or word does not intend to give another an occasion of downfall, but only to satisfy his will' (II-II q.43 a.3 c). Clearly, Aquinas does not use *praeter intentionem* to refer to what one does intend. Yet, some take him to mean that, 'you can in case of necessity kill in self-defence, provided that *in a special theological sense* you do not intend to do so' (Windass 1963, 261, original emphasis). One encounters this idiosyncratic account of intention in Pascal's parody of casuistry found in the seventh of *Les Lettres provinciales*. There Pascal presents his Jesuit's rightly infamous *grande methode de diriger l'intention* (Pascal 1943, 243). According to Pascal's Jesuit, by following this method one can stroll about the dueling green, not intending to fight one's opponent, but intending to walk about. If one's opponent attacks, one may defend oneself. This, following the logic of the method of directing one's intention, would not be dueling.[7] As Elizabeth Anscombe notes, however, such a direction of intention or withholding of intention would itself be intentional (Anscombe 1957, 47). Insofar as Aquinas thinks that intentions have ethical relevance, he must also think that intentions with respect to one's intentions (second-order intentions) also have ethical import. In any

---

[7] For an extended discussion of Pascal's critique see Jonsen and Toulmin (1988), 231–49.

case, Aquinas does not use *praeter intentionem* to refer to a mode of intending, nor does he articulate such a position.

Aquinas does say that what is *praeter intentionem* is *per accidens*. Some interpret him to mean accidental in the sense of accidental consequence. For example, referring to Aquinas's II-II q.64 a.7, Anthony Kenny claims, 'in the context it is not clear whether Aquinas is justifying accidental killing in the course of a struggle or intentional killing when this is the only way to avoid being killed' (Kenny 1973, 140). Yet, in II-II q.64 a.7, Aquinas twice explicitly denies the justifiability of a private individual's intentional killing of an aggressor (in the body of the article and in response to the second objection). Does he mean to speak of an accidental killing?

Imagine pushing, shoving, and pulling an aggressor that results in his death, say, by his tripping, falling, and breaking his neck. Such a death results accidentally, just as someone could die while engaged in friendly horseplay. If this is what Aquinas means when he claims that what is *praeter intentionem* is accidental, then he has brought out an unwieldy concept to attend to what ethicists customarily acknowledge: an agent is not responsible for consequences that accidentally result from an action. Moreover, in article 8, immediately subsequent to that on self-defence, Aquinas asks whether an agent who has killed a man by chance (*casualiter*) is guilty of homicide. His answer? No. This discussion already would have been addressed if what is *praeter intentionem* were *per accidens* in the sense of an accidental consequence. So, both the generally acknowledged point that agents lack responsibility for the accidental consequences of their actions and II-II q.64 a.8 indicate that Thomas does not use *praeter intentionem* to refer to an accidental consequence. Thus, Aquinas does not use *praeter intentionem* to refer to what one directs one's intention away from, nor to what one intends, nor to an accidental consequence. To understand his assertion that what is *praeter intentionem* is *per accidens* requires an investigation of his account of intention.

In I-II q.12 Aquinas considers intention. In q.12 a.1 he claims that 'intention, just as the very word implies, means to tend to something'. Since the will moves the powers of the soul to their appropriate ends, it is evident, Thomas asserts, that intention is an act of the will. He argues that intention is the act of the will with respect to the end, 'as the term towards which something is ordained' (I-II q.12 a.1 ad 4). Aquinas notes that we will the end, health; choose the means, medicine; and intend the complex end-through-means, health-by-means-of-medicine. Intent bears on ends and means. Moreover, intent has moral relevance.

Aquinas proposes a complex evaluation of acts, similar to that which a jeweller employs in assessing a diamond's worth. One evaluates diamonds in terms of their colour, clarity, and cut. Brilliant, dispersed, scintillating colour, perfect clarity, and symmetrical cut constitute a diamond's value. Defects in any one of these aspects diminish and, when severe, render an otherwise priceless diamond worthless. This reflects the Dionysian dictum that goodness is integral; evil, the absence of such integrity, vitiates what otherwise is good (I-II q.19 a.6 ad 1). Thomas proposes that for the ethical assessment of an act, three aspects require attention: what the agent does (the deed or object), the circumstances in which the agent does it (the when, where, how, to whom, and with what), and the end or reason for which the agent acts (I-II q.18 a.1). Of the aspects of an action that make up its integral goodness or its disintegrated badness, the intention of the end is a necessary, but not a sufficient, condition for a complete evaluation of the act.[8]

In light of his account of intention and its role in the analysis of acts, it becomes clear what Aquinas means in asserting that 'moral acts receive their character according to what is intended, not according to what is *praeter intentionem*, for this is *per accidens*'. What is *praeter intentionem* is not essential (as an intention is) in establishing the agent's action as good or as bad. Of course, this does not mean that what is *praeter intentionem* does not enter into the analysis of an act. To see this, one need only note Aquinas's consideration of self-defence. Let us return to that account.

If the assailant's death results from a private individual's justified act of self-defence and the death is neither intended nor accidental, how is the death positively characterized? In II-II q.64 a.7 Aquinas proposes and contrasts two cases of homicidal self-defence: that of an officer of the court and that of a private individual. Thomas holds that a public officer may intend to take the life of his aggressor as long as he uses force proportioned to the end of self-defence (*proportionatus fini*), refers the slaying to the common good, and does not harbour personal animosity against the

---

[8] For an enlightening consideration of Aquinas's action theory, see McInerny (1992).

attacker. In the case of a private individual's justified homicidal self-defence, Thomas permits the slaying of the assailant when it results from the use of force proportioned to self-defence and is not intentional. In both cases the agent must use the minimal force necessary for self-preservation. Only the public official, however, may intentionally kill in self-defence. Consider the following cases. I (a private individual) and my assailant have swords. We begin to fight. I realize that my aggressor has far greater endurance; the only way I can preserve my life is to kill him. According to Thomas, I may not do so because I may not intend his death. Were I an officer of the state, however, I may intentionally kill.

What does Thomas permit to the private individual? When one uses a sword, one risks the attacker's life. This is significant for two reasons. First, although the one defending himself with a sword need not intend to take the life of the aggressor, he does knowingly and willingly risk the aggressor's life. Second (as I shall argue), if intentionally or accidentally killing differs from knowingly and willingly endangering another's life and thereby killing, then there exists a third possibility other than intentional or accidental killing. Namely, there is the assailant's death resulting as a risked consequence.

Intentionally killing differs from risking death. For example, one does not intend to take one's own life when one endangers it. Soldiers, stuntmen, racing-car drivers, police officers, firefighters, and construction workers jeopardize their lives. Do they intend their own deaths? Perhaps some of them do and perhaps some of them ought not so to imperil their lives even when they do not intend to take them. In any case, it would indeed be an eccentric theory of intention that concluded that one who endangered his life thereby intended his death. Similarly, risking another's life is not intending the other's death.

Risked homicide also differs from accidental homicide. In an accidental killing, the agent inculpably does not foresee the death. For example, when at one's barbeque a friend suffers a lethal allergic reaction to grilled swordfish, one kills him accidentally. When death results from endangering someone's life, however, the reasonable agent foresees the death as a possible consequence. Accordingly, when one kills someone accidentally, one lacks responsibility for his death; when one kills someone whose life one has knowingly endangered, one has responsibility. Thus, killing someone accidentally differs from killing someone whose life one has knowingly endangered.

I risk the assailant's life when I do not intend to take it, but chance it in self-defence. I am more willing to preserve my life than I am to forgo hazarding my aggressor's. Aquinas argues for the permissibility of such an act. He proposes that while a private individual may not intend to take the life of an assailant, he may risk killing the aggressor by defending himself with such force that the aggressor's death is a foreseeable consequence. This interpretation accords with what Aquinas himself implies when he asserts that 'the act of fornication or of adultery is not ordered to the conservation of one's own life out of necessity as is the act from which sometimes (*quando-que*) follows homicide' (II-II q.64 a.7 ad 4). As he uses it in q.64 a.7, Aquinas restricts *praeter intentionem* to what occurs sometimes.[9] He does not consider the foresight of an inevitable consequence. Yet, in standard contemporary double-effect cases (for example, tactical bombing that harms non-combatants) one foresees harm as an inevitable consequence. In this respect, Aquinas's originating account significantly differs from what DER has become. Nonetheless, one discerns the core of DER in his treatment of self-defence. First, an exceptionless moral norm leads to a hard case. Second, intention plays a crucial role in the evaluation of the act. Third, although Aquinas does not, one may abstract the following permissive criteria from Thomas's treatment:

1. The act is the least harmful capable of achieving the end (*proportionatus fini*);
2. considered independently of the evil effect, the act is permissible;
3. the agent is more obliged to pursue the good than to avoid the evil (*plus tenetur*); and
4. the agent intends the good and does not intend the evil as a means or as an end.[10]

Of course, to speak of these elements present in Aquinas's account as criteria implies their generalizability. While

[9] Objecting to this interpretation, one might argue that *quandoque* refers not to homicidal self-defence, but to self-defence in general. Thus, Thomas would be noting that self-defence is justified, even though the death of the aggressor sometimes follows from acts of self-defence. This, however, is a non-starter. For the question is whether homicidal self-defence is justified, not whether self-defence *simpliciter* is justified. Certain conditions obtaining, Aquinas holds that a private individual's act of self-defence that is sometimes homicidal is justified.

[10] For an alternative consideration of the criteria involved in Aquinas's treatment of double effect see Matthews (1999).

Aquinas does not generalize them, one discerns his use of a similar approach in his discussion of scandal, to which I now turn.

Prior to his discussion of homicidal self-defence, Thomas considers scandal (II-II, q.43). Following St Jerome, he understands scandal to be words or deeds that occasion another's spiritual ruin. Homicide harms another's corporeal life; scandal, his spiritual life. Accordingly, scandal harms another more gravely. Like homicide, however, certain instances of scandal occur *praeter intentionem* of the agent. Moreover, scandal may occur *praeter conditionem* of the agent's deed (II-II q.43 a.1 ad 4). That is, the agent does not intend the word or deed to be an occasion of spiritual harm and the word or deed is not of the type to be of spiritual harm. With respect to harm being besides the condition of the act, Aquinas excludes sinful acts and acts that appear sinful. For these deeds are of the type to cause spiritual harm to another. Spiritual harm resulting from deeds that are neither sinful nor appear sinful occurs *praeter conditionem*. With these distinctions, Aquinas defines passive scandal as spiritual harm that occurs besides the intent of the agent and besides the nature of the act. In contrast, he defines active scandal as a deed or word intended or of the kind to cause spiritual harm. One cannot justify active scandal. Giving passive scandal, however, may be justified on the part of the one whose (otherwise blameless) word or deed occasions another's harm. (It cannot be justified on the part of the one scandalized, for he fails spiritually.) In II-II q.43 a.7 Aquinas asks if one should forgo spiritual goods in order to avoid scandal; in the following article he asks the same question concerning temporal goods. While his answers to the two questions differ in their specifics, Aquinas holds that one may by word or deed cause spiritual harm to another when the good at issue has great enough importance and cannot be secured absent the scandal. For example, he says that, since 'a man ought to love his own salvation more than another's', he ought not to forgo spiritual goods necessary for his salvation to avoid scandalizing another. (This duty appears parallel to one's obligation (of q.64 a.7) to take greater care of one's own corporeal life than that of another.) One sees in his discussion of passive scandal the lineaments of an account akin to that of II-II q.64 a.7 and found in the above-noted four criteria which Aquinas himself does not explicitly generalize. As will become evident, Aquinas's seminal position develops from individual cases into general principles induced from those cases that, in turn, serve as criteria to make deductions about specific cases. In short, in the history of double effect one sees the mind's inductive progression from the particular to the general.

1.2.   DEVELOPMENTS OF THOMAS'S ACCOUNT

Joseph Mangan (1949) and J. Ghoos (1951) independently address the historical development of double effect after Aquinas. Mangan emphasizes II-II q.64 a.7 and the role of the Carmelite Domingo de Sta Teresa who wrote the tract (published in 1647) *De vitiis et peccatis* (Salmanticensis 1877 edn., vii) in which one finds double-effect criteria presented as general principles. Differing from Mangan, Ghoos proposes that double effect receives its first full formation in the Dominican John of St Thomas's (John Poinsot's) tract entitled *De bonitate et malitia actuum humanorum*. This commentary on Aquinas's I-II qs. 18–21—the most relevant text is q.20 a.5 where Aquinas considers the ethical import of an act's consequences—was published posthumously in 1645 in the fourth volume of the *Cursus theologicus* (Poinsot 1885 edn., v and vi). Poinsot wrote only the first four volumes and the first part of the fifth of this work which was initially divided into eight volumes and published between 1637 and 1667. He addresses q.20 a.5 at length in dispute 11, article 6, numbers 30–46 (Poinsot 1885 edn., vi). With the observations of Mangan and Ghoos in mind, one notes that double effect appears explicitly (albeit inchoately) in II-II q.64 a.7 and implicitly in I-II q.20 a.5. Moreover, one need not regard either Domingo de Sta Teresa or John of St Thomas as the thinker who definitively articulates double effect. Rather, they and their predecessors belong to the Thomistic tradition which serves as the matrix of double-effect reasoning.

The first thinker in that tradition who reiterates and expands the set of cases in which one discerns double effect is St Antoninus, archbishop of Florence (1389–1459), whose four-part *Summa theologica moralis*, published posthumously, went through fifteen editions within fifty years of its initial Venetian appearance of 1477. Antoninus repeats Aquinas's use of double-effect criteria in his consideration of both self-defence and scandal. He extends double

effect to include the case of alluring dress. Antoninus interprets Aquinas concerning attractive dress as Aquinas interprets Augustine on self-defence. That is, Aquinas
understands Augustine to forbid the intent to kill in self-
defence but not acts of double effect; similarly, Antoninus
interprets Aquinas as prohibiting dress intended to provoke
lust, but not dress by which one intends to attract the opposite sex while foreseeing that it will provoke lust.

The relevant text in Aquinas is II-II q.169, entitled 'concerning modesty insofar as it consists in outward apparel'.
Aquinas proposes that a wife or an unmarried woman who
dresses attractively to please a husband or to attract a potential husband does not act badly. A woman, however, who
neither has nor seeks a spouse would act wrongly in so
dressing. (He holds the same concerning men.) Thomas
does not explicitly refer to the intent of the one who adorns
herself, although his 'in order thereby to please her husband'
draws attention to intent just as he proposes (in his q.64 a.7
discussion of homicide) that Augustine's 'for the sake of
these things' implies intent. Antoninus, citing Aquinas's
text, proposes that one must consider the intent of the one
who dresses and the dress itself (Antoninus 1959, vol. ii, t. iv,
c. v, vii, 595). Antoninus holds that when the intent of the
woman is to please her husband, to avoid disgrace, or to
attract a husband, then she does not act wrongly. With
respect to clothing itself, Antoninus distinguishes between
apparel itself being the occasion of lust or being taken as an
occasion of lust. If a woman were to wear decorous dress
appropriate to her status and country that men took as an
occasion to lust, she would not be at fault (nor would, as it

were, her clothing). He holds that when a woman does not intend to provoke lust and her attire comports with her status and local customs, then she acts permissibly. One here encounters a case of double effect which becomes a classic of moral theology, variations of which one finds in most subsequent casuists, including Cajetan, Suarez, and John of St Thomas: the beautiful young woman out for a walk who provokes impure desire in bystanders. Antoninus reiterates Aquinas, expands the repertoire of double-effect cases, and exemplifies a sensitivity to the problem of good becoming entangled with evil and thereby requiring moral analysis to separate the otherwise inextricable.

Like Antoninus, Tommaso de Vio Gaetani (Cajetan, 1469–1534) closely follows Aquinas, their fellow Dominican. Cardinal Cajetan wrote the first and most influential in a long line of commentaries on Thomas's *Summa theologiae*. In his commentary (published in 1517) on the II-II, Cajetan interprets Aquinas in q.64 a.7 as holding that causally necessary effects need not be intended. He reiterates Thomas's position that intent has essential moral import while what falls beside intent has less significance. To illustrate the point Cajetan offers an enduring quotidian example. A physician intends health by means of medicine, but he need not intend the causally necessitated weakness that follows from otherwise healthful medicine (Cajetan 1891–9, vol. ix, q.64 a.7, 74). Today, one thinks of the oncologist who intends to restore health by means of chemotherapy that also nauseates, weakens, and causes hair-loss. Cajetan expands upon Aquinas's discussion of a private individual's homicidal self-defence, considering whether one may with foresight kill in defence of important property. He thinks one may. Considering the (according to him, permissible) case of a judge sentencing a man he knows to be innocent extra-judicially, he holds more generally that otherwise legitimate and necessary acts for the common good may result in the deaths of the innocent, absent the intent to kill. To intend to kill the innocent, however, violates all laws (ibid., q.67 a.2, 100). He refers back to the double-effect case of self-defence and extends this account to what the judge does. Although he does not consider it specifically, non-combatant casualties in war serve as the classic illustration of a public official's act that results in the foreseen but not intended deaths of the innocent. In his commentary on I-II q.20 a.5 (where Aquinas discusses whether a foreseen effect adds to the goodness or badness of an action), Cajetan holds that foreseen bad effects do not make otherwise good acts bad. He offers as examples a beautiful woman going for a walk and thereby eliciting lust, Christ revealing himself as the Messiah and thereby provoking disbelief, and an individual defending himself against an aggressor and thereby killing him (ibid., vol. vi, q.20 a.5, 162). Cajetan develops DER by linking Aquinas's treatment of I-II q.20 with II-II q.64 a.7 and gathering together a number of cases to which he applies such reasoning.

Cajetan's commentary on Aquinas's work indicates the significance of the latter's insight for theologians. Yet, as general of the Dominican Order from 1508 to 1518, he reaffirmed the venerable tradition (to which Aquinas belonged as a student and teacher) that theological instruction use Peter Lombard's *Sentences*. Accordingly, Cajetan's fellow Dominican Francisco de Vitoria, while a student teaching at the Sorbonne, would have followed that mandate even as he, following Cajetan's example, began to orient theological studies around Aquinas's work. At Paris prior to his 1526 election to the primary chair of theology at the University of Salamanca, Vitoria edited and wrote prefaces to Aquinas's II-II of the *Summa theologiae* (in 1512) and to Antoninus's *Summa theologiae moralis* (in 1521). In these early projects of editing other's work instead of authoring his own, he exemplified a self-effacing attitude which persisted throughout his life of scholarship. When asked why he did not write more, he is reputed to have said, 'my students have enough to read'. Indeed, were it not for his insistence that students take notes and their diligence in doing so, we might have little attributable to Vitoria. Amongst lectures faithfully recorded number his discussion of Aquinas's II-II q.64 a.7.

Vitoria's interpretation approximates Cajetan's. Both hold that what one intends differs ethically from causally necessitated outcomes associated with what one intends. While (as noted above) Cajetan implies that he would employ double effect to judge the permissibility of harming noncombatants in a just war, Vitoria explicitly addresses such a case in his discussion of q.64 a.6, where he holds that soldiers may kill innocents when it is incidental to attacking a legitimate target, yet they may not intentionally kill the innocent (Vitoria 1997, 191). Commenting on q.64 a.5, he proposes that one may forego what one needs in order to live thereby to provide for another even if one foreseeably perishes (ibid. 177). While he does not induce general prin-

ciples, he continues the trajectory Aquinas initiates and
expands the cases to include the perennially cited instance
of non-combatant casualties.

After Vitoria's death in 1546 an illustrious line of Dominicans occupied the primary chair of theology at Salamanca. His immediate successors were Melchior Cano,
Dominic de Soto, Peter de Sotomayor, and John Mancio.
During the last decade of Vitoria's life, a new religious order
arrived on the scene, the Society of Jesus, or Jesuits. Three
decades after Vitoria's death, the influential Jesuit theologian, Francis Suarez (1548–1617) studied theology at the
University of Salamanca under John Mancio (1497–1576).
Suarez continues the (thus far) Dominican tradition of
DER, addressing the following scenarios: the incidental kill-
ing of innocents during war, putting oneself in mortal danger for a just cause, selling an otherwise legitimate item that
will be abused, and the woman whose beauty provokes lust
as she goes about her business.[11] By addressing these cases,
Suarez ensures that the line of thought initiated by the
Dominicans pollinates the new and increasingly influential
Society of Jesus.

Historians relate that Suarez was probably seen but not
heard by John of St Thomas (John Poinsot). Poinsot's studies at the University of Coimbre (1604–16) coincided with
Suarez's tenure as primary chair of theology, which began in
1597 and ended two decades later with his death. Poinsot
offers a set of cases similar to that found in Suarez, to which

[11] Found, respectively, in Suarez (1856) xii, tract. 3, disp. 13, sect. 7,
ns. 15–19; xxiii, disp. 46, sect. 2, n. 2; xii, tract. 2, disp. 10, sect. 4, ns. 4–6;
and xii, tract. 2, disp 10, sect. 3, n. 10.

he adds the case of necessary food consumed that incidentally causes venereal pleasure. One finds these considerations in the posthumously published (1645) fourth volume of his *Cursus theologicus*. Here, like his fellow Dominican Cajetan before him, John of St Thomas comments on Aquinas's consideration of the moral significance of the effects of one's acts (I-II q.20 a.5). As noted, Ghoos (1951) proposes that one first finds a general account of double effect explicitly enunciated in this work. Yet, as we have seen, John of St Thomas continues in the Thomistic tradition of the preceding two centuries. Poinsot died in 1644; like his namesake, he did so on a journey while far from his convent and confrères.

It was in 1647 that other monks, the Carmelites of Salamanca and Alcala, published the tract entitled *De vitiis et peccatis* in their *Cursus theologicus*. Domingo de Sta Teresa wrote this treatise, which Mangan refers to as 'the most outstanding link in the further development of the principle of the double effect... which joins the recognition of the principle as applied to particular sections of moral theology and the recognition of the principle as a general principle applicable to the whole field of moral theology' (Mangan 1949, 56). Domingo de Sta Teresa explicitly understands there to be a generalizable set of permissibility conditions applicable to a set of acts causing good and evil. With respect to the set of acts to which these conditions apply, he excludes acts evil in themselves, such as lying, adultery, and theft. He also rules out acts in which the good effect is brought about solely by means of the evil effect and acts that have only an evil effect. Excluding such acts from consideration, he holds that an act causing good and evil is permissible if:

1. there is a proportionately serious good effect; that
2. (*a*) precedes the permitted evil or (*b*) follows with equal immediacy from the act;
3. the permitted evil is foreseen, not intended; and
4. one cannot omit the good effect without significant hardship.[12]

One notes a number of points concerning these criteria. First, they incorporate an understandable caution which manifests itself as redundancy. (As I argue in section 1.3, a complete account of condition 3 captures the import of 2*a* and *b*.) While not appealing in terms of economy and simplicity, this redundancy makes pedagogical sense. Domingo de Sta Teresa concerns himself not with philosophical elegance and economy, but with the direction of troubled consciences. A critical reader notes that he writes as a manualist. Like a good technical writer, he builds in a thoroughgoing redundancy to ensure against error. Second, one might initially think that condition 1 (proportionately serious good effect) equates to 4 (one cannot omit the good effect without grave inconvenience). However, condition 1 compares the good to the evil of this act while 4 compares the good of this act to what obtains when one forgoes the act. Thinking of condition 4, we imagine not acting. Of course, meeting the demand of 4 partially depends upon

---

[12] Here I follow Mangan (1949), 56–7.

how good the good at issue is. This stands at the centre of condition 1. Nonetheless, 1 and 4 differ, for they ask us to think about different, albeit allied, considerations. Third, while perseveration may be the mark of a good teacher, error is not. Speaking of 'permitting' the evil will not do. For the acts at issue cause evil. For example, one kills non-combatants in war. Although Domingo de Sta Teresa speaks of permitting evil, he applies double effect to cases of causing evil. (In section 5.2 I consider cases of allowing.) Understandably, yet erroneously, he appears to try to diminish the gravity of what he argues for (as a permissible causing of evil) by speaking of it as if it were a permissible permitting of evil. The unhappy phrase 'permitting the evil effect' chronically plagues articulations of double effect (as will become more evident in section 3.1, which attends to this and other terminological pitfalls). Nonetheless, Domingo de Sta Teresa presents a generalized account and a set of cases from which that account derives.

Two further thinkers deserve attention before turning to the contemporary period: John de Lugo and St Alphonsus Liguori. Like others in the development of double effect, the Jesuit de Lugo studied at the University of Salamanca. His *De justitia et jure* of 1642, which he personally presented to Pope Urban VIII, earned him the red hat of a cardinal. In that work he presents the memorable double-effect example of someone fleeing on horseback from an unjust pursuer down a narrow alley in which lies an infant who will be killed if the rider continues. De Lugo holds that one may flee down the alley. For if the infant were absent what one does is not bad in itself; rather, one wills the good of self-preservation. Similarly, when the infant is present one intends self-preservation, one does not intend the evil effect, and the good of one's preservation follows as immediately as the infant's death. He proposes this case as illustrative of the permissibility of a pregnant woman having a tumor removed when such surgery will result in the death of the baby. He articulates the reasoning classically applied to the hysterectomy of a gravid uterus. Moreover, de Lugo notes the existence of a rule that is 'difficult to apply to particular cases' (de Lugo 1868–9, vol. vi, dispute x, sect. v, n. 124).

Of John de Lugo, Ligouri (a Doctor of the Catholic Church) said, 'after Saint Thomas, easily the principal theologian'. Accordingly, when Liguori considers cases of acts that foreseeably kill the innocent (such as a woman taking a drug to preserve her life knowing that it will cause the death of her foetus), he initially cites Aquinas's treatment of q.64 a.7 and de Lugo's passage about the infant in the narrow alley (Liguori 1954 vol. i, l. iii, tract iv, c. i, n. 393, 643). Showing a tendency of eighteenth-century thinkers noted by Mangan, Liguori presents a very abbreviated treatment of double effect as a general approach to certain cases (ibid., vol. ii, l. v, tract. *Praeambulus*, xiv, 692). He cites Aquinas's general discussion of the voluntary and the moral relevance of the effects of acts (found in I-II qs. 6 and 20). At the end of the eighteenth century Ligouri presents cases of double effect and recognizes it as a general approach to such cases.

Turning to the nineteenth century, one finds a fully generalized presentation of double effect. Chief amongst its proponents stands the Jesuit moral theologian Jean-Pierre

Gury. In his 1850 *Compendium theologiae moralis* (which went on to seventeen editions during his lifetime) one encounters the contemporary version of double-effect reasoning and a recognition of its past (Gury cites relevant texts in Aquinas, Alphonsus, and de Lugo). He asserts a principle bearing upon the permissibility of acts having good and evil effects. He understands the principle to have four conditions:

1. The ultimate end of the author must be good, that is, the author may not intend the evil effect, because otherwise he would intend something evil...

2. The cause itself of the effects must be good or at least indifferent...For, if the cause is evil in itself, of itself it makes the action imputable as a fault.

3. The evil effect must not be the means to the good effect. The reason is that, if the cause directly produces the evil effect and produces the good effect only by means of the evil effect, then the good is sought by willing the evil. And it is never lawful to do evil, no matter how slight, in order that good may come of it...

4. There must be a proportionately serious reason for actuating the cause, so that the author of the action would not be obliged by any virtue to omit the action. For natural equity obliges us to avoid evil and prevent harm from coming to our neighbor when we can do so without proportionately serious loss to ourselves. (Mangan 1949, 60–1)

While the substance of these conditions has remained the same as that articulated by Gury, they have come to be ordered and expressed in the following manner:

1. the act in itself is good or indifferent;
2. the agent intends the good effect and not the evil effect;
3. the good effect is not produced by the evil effect; and
4. there is a proportionately grave reason for causing the evil effect.

Typically, proponents of DER concatenate these as four necessary conditions that jointly suffice to permit an act causing good and evil.

As we have seen, thinkers arrived at the general criteria Gury proposes by means of an induction Aquinas initiated. Over the six centuries separating Aquinas and Gury, thinkers in the Thomistic tradition expanded the number of cases considered in DER and further articulated its grounds in action theory, arriving at the criteria as generally applicable to relevant cases. In what follows, I consider these criteria, their import, order, relation to one another, necessity, and sufficiency.

1.3.   SIMPLIFYING THE RECEIVED CRITERIA

The first criterion, that an act be good or indifferent, rules out the application of double effect to otherwise bad acts having good and bad effects. For example, Robin Hood's intrinsically bad act of stealing has the good effect of relieving the poor and the bad effect of disconcerting the rich.

However, as a wrongful taking, it is not a candidate for DER. Accordingly, one states the first criterion as: (1) the act considered independently of its bad effect is not wrong.

The idea of an act wrong in itself has a venerable history. Speaking of such acts in the *Ethics* dedicated to his son Nicomachus, Aristotle asserts:

> the names of some automatically include baseness, e.g., spite, shamelessness, envy [among feelings], and adultery, theft, murder, among actions. All of these and similar things are called by these names because they themselves, not their excesses or deficiencies, are base. Hence in doing these things we can never be correct, but must invariably be in error. We cannot do them well or not well— e.g. by committing adultery with the right woman at the right time in the right way; on the contrary, it is true unconditionally that to do any of them is to be in error. (Aristotle 1985, 45)

Double-effect reasoning does not justify acts that have wrongness built into them. Rather, situated in an ethic acknowledging such acts, it excludes them from the set of acts the permissibility of which it considers.

Would it be right to say that double effect prohibits such acts? DER is a set of criteria. Its first criterion echoes the impermissibility of intrinsically wrong acts. Not considering such acts, the other criteria prohibit (when not met). Over-archingly, double effect functions permissively while its elements taken separately exert prohibitive force.

The first condition differs from the others. For it solely restates the moral commitments that lead one to have recourse to DER, while the remaining conditions refine and show the further import of those commitments. The first condition excludes the application of the remaining conditions to acts impermissible in kind. Since it makes no sense to consider the permissibility of such acts, the first condition appropriately comes first.

The second condition (that the agent intends the good and not the evil) stands at the centre of double-effect reasoning. As earlier noted, Aquinas holds that there are three basic characteristics of an act's ethical status: the agent's intended end-via-means, the deed done, and the circumstances within which the agent does the deed and seeks the end. There is the why (end) and how (means) of intent, the what of deed, and the amalgam (where, when, to whom, with what, in what manner, and so on) of circumstances. The second condition instances a commitment to the ethical relevance of intent. Intent is complex, bearing upon means and ends, causes and effects. With respect to ends and means, the second condition positively requires and negatively excludes certain intents on the agent's part. Thus, the full import of the second condition is that the agent intends the good and does not intend the evil, neither as his means nor as his end. In the case of justified tactical bombing, the bomber intends the good of victory as his end. If the bomber were not to intend victory, but fame, then dropping the bombs would be an act of vanity, and not justifiable. Moreover, the bomber may not intend the deaths and harm done to the non-combatants as an end nor as a means to victory. The second condition appropriately comes second. For as the first rules out deeds that cannot be permitted, the second focuses on the intent of the agent in virtue of which an otherwise permissible deed is good or bad. Of course, much more needs and shall be said regarding the second condition.

Many understand the third condition (the good effect is not produced by the evil effect) to mean that the evil effect may not cause the good effect. For, according to this line of reasoning, then the agent would intend the evil as a means to the good.[13] So understood, the third condition rules out the bad effect's causing the good.[14] One issue in considering the third criterion concerns the relation between causes and effects on the one hand, and ends and means on the other. An agent intends and seeks an end as something he wants for its own sake; an agent intends a means as something he wants for the sake of an end. One might say that an agent wants an end in itself and for itself, while he wants a means in itself but not for itself. In terms of the agent, his wanting of the end causes his wanting of the means. In terms of realizing the agent's plan, however, the causal relations reverse: the means cause the end. Indeed, the agent wants the means only insofar as they cause the end. In order for something to be a means, it must cause an end. We may conclude that, if x is a means to y, then x causes y. We may not conclude, however, that if x causes y, then x is a means to y. For, in order to do so, we need to focus on the causal relations found in an agent's wanting of x and of y. If the agent wants y and wants x insofar as it causes y, then we can say that x is a means to y. This brief consideration of the relation between cause/effect and means/end serves as a basis to address the difficulty with the third condition.

Interpreted charitably, the third condition appears redun-

[13] See e.g. Oderberg (2000), 91.
[14] Some advocates assert that the good must temporally precede the evil or must be as immediate as the evil. See Davis (1946), 13–4.

dant. For, when one understands it as asserting that the agent may not intend the evil effect as a means or as an end, it replicates the second condition. Read less charitably, it seems erroneous. For, when understood to rule out the causing of the good by the evil effect, it leads to error. To see this, consider the classic double-effect case of tactical bombing. Imagine an otherwise justified case of such bombing in which the deaths of the non-combatants partially cause the victory the bomber seeks (say that the enemy population regards the non-combatants's deaths as an unacceptable cost of war and this in part leads them to surrender). Since the tactical bomber does not seek to kill the non-combatants, such an act would not thereby be ruled out by double effect, although the non-combatants's deaths in part cause victory. For, contrary to the less charitable reading of the third condition, double-effect reasoning focuses on the casual relations between the good and evil effects only insofar as the agent intends them. As noted above, that something is a means entails that it is a cause, but that something is a cause does not entail that it is a means. Of course, if the evil effect were the only cause of the good effect, then (if the agent knew this, and so on) one might reasonably conclude that the agent intended the evil as a means.[15] This, of course, would be ruled out by condition 2. Thus, even when so understood as ruling out the evil effect as being the only means to the good, condition 3 merely reiterates condition

---

[15] Domingo de Sta Teresa explicitly excludes cases in which the bad effect is the only cause of the good (Mangan 1949, 57).

2. Accordingly, it is superfluous. Moreover, in classic double-effect cases such as tactical bombing the evil effect may partially cause the good effect. The third criterion ought to be abandoned as either redundant or erroneous.

The fourth condition asks us to compare one's reasons for doing the good to one's reasons for avoiding the evil. If one's reasons for causing the good have proportionate gravity, one may act. This criterion appears consequentialist. For this reason, in debates concerning double effect the fourth criterion receives little attention. For consequentialists comprise the typical opponents of double effect. Since the fourth condition readily admits of a consequentialist interpretation in which one weighs outcomes and opts for the greatest good, little controversy surrounds it. Clearly, however, the fact that other conditions must be satisfied before it has a role to play indicates that it serves a non-consequentialist ethic. (Indeed, as the reader will note in, for example, sections 4.2.3 and 4.3, consequentialists contest precisely the need to satisfy those other criteria.) Other than its place, however, ought one to interpret the fourth condition in a consequentialist manner?

Yes and no. Certainly, the relative amounts of good and evil figure prominently as reasons. Numbers count. The fourth criterion incorporates this truth. It goes beyond it, however, by admitting that some things that one cannot count still do matter. Consider the agent's relation to the goods and evils at issue. For example, recall Aquinas's claim that one has a greater obligation to preserve one's own life than another's. From a purely consequentialist standpoint, however, one's own self being alive is as good as another's. If one interpreted the fourth condition as involving only a numeric comparison, the proportion (in Aquinas's example) would be 1 : 1. It is not. Thus, the proportionateness of the fourth condition includes, without being limited to, sheer quantitative comparison. Obligations that attend one's role, as, for example, a mother, brother, friend, wife, fireman, teacher, doctor, soldier, or fellow countryman, partially constitute proportionately grave reasons. Consequences count. Obligations matter. Both comprise proportionately grave reasons.

Duly noting that one cannot entirely capture the fourth condition in either consequentialist or deontological terms, proportionately grave reasons require further articulation. To do so, I propose as a useful foil a flat-footed counting of outcomes. (Consequentialists do *not* compare upshots in this unsophisticated way; indeed, ingenious systems of counting characterize that account.) Imagine foreseeably but not intentionally killing non-combatants while tactically bombing an artillery installation. Stipulate that the act satisfies the other criteria. The evils at issue (the terrorizing and killing of non-combatants) do not outweigh the goods (ending the lethal threat of the artillery, victory over the unjust enemy, self-preservation, self-determination). Thus interpreted, the fourth criterion permits such an act. Yet, what if there were some other, less harmful, way of bombing that would mitigate or entirely remove the evil? For example, what if different types of bombs, a different time, or a different approach would lessen or remove the harm?

Clearly, it would be wrong to cause gratuitous harm.[16] Insofar as the realization that one ought to avoid evil underlies recourse to double effect, it would be odd, indeed perverse, to interpret the fourth condition as holding that evil is not to be eliminated or mitigated, when practically possible. The entire tenor of and motivation for double effect indicates that proportionate gravity includes a consideration of both the contemplated harm's necessity and, given its necessity, the opportunities for mitigation. With respect to tactical bombing, proportionately grave reasons properly understood exclude unnecessary harm while requiring the lessening of any necessary harm. Recall Aquinas's account. He asserts that the permissible act of homicidal self-defence must be *proportionatus fini*, proportioned to its end. He notes the impermissibility of using more violence than necessary. Indeed, given the common use of the phrase 'a proportionately serious reason' in the fourth condition, one might think that advocates conjoin Aquinas's *proportionatus fini* with the quantitative relation between the good and evil. Aquinas speaks to the quantitative relation between the good and harm when he says 'one is more obliged to care for one's own life than for that of another'. With *proportionatus fini* he attends to the necessity of the harm (in his account, the necessity of risking the harm) to the achieve-

---

[16] By gratuitous harm I refer to concomitant harm that is not necessary. The tactical bomber, for example, causes concomitant harm that is not necessary if, either: (1) he destroys the artillery with the children present while, other things being equal, he could so in their absence, or (2) he cannot destroy the installation while the children are absent, but he uses bombs that cause greater concomitant harm while having less concomitantly harmful, otherwise effective bombs available.

ment of the good. Thus, one notes two issues. First, the good must be greater. Second, the harm must not be gratuitous. That is, it must be the least harm necessary.

Yet, what does one assert by saying that the permissible act will be the least harmful necessary? Clearly, there are acts that would not harm at all; for example, when the tactical bomber chooses not to bomb. Of course, it must be the least harmful act of those acts capable of achieving the good. So, for example, if we were to have a choice of more and less precise bombs, we would choose the more precise. Indeed, in the development of weapons, one of the criteria that ought to be attended to would be the mitigation and elimination of concomitant harm. Of otherwise comparable weapons, those causing less collateral harm ought to be preferred. A country that chose not to develop or to use such weapons resorts to double effect disingenuously. Those who have real cases of conscience sincerely want to avoid evil. Accordingly, they take practical measures to do so.

What costs must the agent bear in order to mitigate or eliminate the harm? Perhaps if one devoted enough resources to their development, one could invent extraordinarily precise, powerfully destructive weapons that eliminate concomitant damage. Again, sticking with the tactical-bombing case, must the bomber bear risks in order to minimize the death and destruction he causes to the non-combatants? For example, when flying at a lower altitude (and, therefore, at greater risk from anti-aircraft batteries) causes less concomitant harm, is he obligated to do so? Most advocates of double effect have not addressed this question. Michael Walzer, who has, holds that when applicable, as in tactical-bombing cases, the agent must bear risks in order to minimize the harm. Walzer modifies the intent condition, holding that 'the intention of the actor is good, that is, he aims narrowly at the acceptable effect; the evil effect is not one of his ends, nor is it a means to his ends, and, aware of the evil involved, he seeks to minimize it, accepting costs to himself' (Walzer 1977, 155). Walzer holds that due care must be taken to minimize the harm. By due care, he means that in a case such as tactical bombing where the agent must bear risks to himself, the risks would be limited to those that do not doom the enterprise to failure. Due care is a prudential matter about which reasonable people reasonably disagree. Must one, as Walzer holds, act as French pilots did in World War II when bombing occupied France, and bomb from low altitudes which increases the risk to the pilot and crew while decreasing the danger to non-combatants? Is it permissible to bomb in a less risky, more harmful manner (while still satisfying the proportionality condition)? Certainly, unnecessary harming must be excluded, even when the good is greater than the evil. So, for example, if the importance to victory of a military target were to justify killing schoolchildren near the military installation, and with no added costs one can destroy the installation without killing the children, one must do so. To do otherwise would be to kill the children gratuitously. On the other hand, if the only way one could avoid killing the children were a suicide mission, one would not be obliged so to act. In between these two extremes one finds due care. In any case, DER excludes gratuitous harming while requiring due care to mitigate evil.

The traditional four conditions of double effect can be simplified. Moreover, the latent exclusion of unnecessary harming can be made explicit, as in Aquinas's originating account. So simplified, one may state double-effect reasoning as permitting an act causing good and evil when it meets the following conditions:

1. the act considered independently of its evil effect is not in itself wrong;
2. the agent intends the good and does not intend the evil either as an end or as a means; and,
3. the agent has proportionately grave reasons for acting, addressing his relevant obligations, comparing the consequences, and, considering the necessity of the evil, exercising due care to eliminate or mitigate it.

A number of allied questions bear upon the acts to which one applies double effect. Does 'double' mean two and only two effects? Clearly, it is to be understood qualitatively, not quantitatively. That is, in those cases to which one applies DER, there are qualitatively two effects: good and bad. Quantitatively, there may be myriad good and bad effects; for example, in the terminal-sedation case: the relief of pain, the relief of the family, the death of the patient, the grief of the family, and so on. In addition to the number of the effects, there is also the question of their probabilities. Typically, DER cases receiving the greatest attention concern an agent causing some good foreseeing with certitude that he will also cause some evil. Such cases receive attention as they test the tenability of double effect most completely. Other things being equal, when one can justify causing harm with certitude, all the more may one justify risking harm. Yet, would it be justifiable to cause harm with certitude if the good effect were less than certain? For example, could one tactically bomb an artillery installation when certain that doing so would kill non-combatants while not being certain that one would destroy the installation? In such cases, the third condition comparing the effects at issue would reasonably include their relative probabilities. Thus, double effect bears on cases in which the probabilities of the good and evil differ. Yet, one odd implication of this appears to be that double effect applies in cases in which there may be fewer than two actually realized qualitatively distinct effects. For, if the good or evil effect were not certain, then one might cause the one effect without bringing about the other. Is this right? Going back to the origin of double effect in Aquinas, it seems that this implication was present from the beginning. For, as argued earlier, he holds that it is permissible to risk killing the assailant while defending one's own life. This may have two effects (the death of the aggressor and the preservation of one's own life); or it may result in only one effect (the preservation of one's own life without the death of the aggressor). Thus, an act justified by double effect need not result in two effects. Given these preliminaries, let us now turn our attention to the most prominent contemporary accounts of DER.

2

The contemporary conversation

In the previous chapter I presented the historical background of double-effect reasoning. I now consider contemporary offshoots of DER, such as proportionalism; alternatives, such as Alan Donagan's casuistry of material guilt and Frances Kamm's non-absolutist Principle of Permissible Harm; and recent presentations of double effect, such as that of Warren Quinn and the trio of Finnis, Grisez, and Boyle.

2.1. PROPORTIONALISM

Before considering current anti-consequentialist replacements, revisions, and versions of DER, I turn to a radical transformation of double effect that has recently arisen in Catholic moral theology, the provenance of DER. I speak of proportionalism. Proportionalism transmutes DER into a consequentialist position.[1] Consequentialism serves as the

---

[1] The objections of proportionalists notwithstanding, philosophers uniformly consider proportionalism a version of consequentialism, as Frankena notes (1978), 159.

genus for those ethical theories that propose the right act to be that which produces the greatest net good consequences. The species of consequentialism differ from one another to the extent to which they understand good and evil (or, more technically, value and disvalue) differently. Accordingly, proportionalism differs from other consequentialist accounts in terms of what it counts as good and bad in evaluating an act. While other accounts might consider pleasure and pain or the satisfaction or dissatisfaction of one's subjective preferences as good and bad, proportionalism takes into account what it regards as objectively grounded values and disvalues. So, for example, proportionalism counts sterilization or the death of a person as objective disvalues, independently of one's preferences regarding these states of affairs or the pleasure and pain associated with them. Proportionalism regards values such as a person being alive, healthy, and happy to be objectively grounded insofar as God creates humans to be so. In this respect, proportionalism may be properly thought of as a theistic ethic, or a moral theology. Because of its insistence on objective values and disvalues grounded in the world as God means it to be, one might think that it would be welcomed by the Roman Catholic Church as a considerable improvement over the typically more subjective and secular versions of consequentialism that dominate much contemporary thinking. In this understandable assumption, however, one would be mistaken. For proportionalism shares the common consequentialist commitment that acts cannot be characterized as wrong independently of their consequences. Orthodox Catholic moral theology, however, holds that acts can be judged as wrong in themselves, or as intrinsically wrong. For example, consider a husband's vasectomy for contraceptive purposes. A proportionalist would argue that a man's being sterile is an objective evil. For, as created, a male has an ordination towards procreation. On this point, proportionalism and doctrinal Roman Catholicism agree. The proportionalist would argue, however, that the objective evil of being sterilized can be outweighed by the objective goods of enjoying sexual pleasure and devoting more resources to one's current children. In effect, the proportionalist holds that, while objectively evil, sterilization and disparate other acts are not in themselves or intrinsically wrong. It is on this latter point concerning acts wrong in themselves that Roman Catholic dogma and proportionalism differ. For this reason, although proportionalism grounds values in the world as God means it to be, the Roman Catholic Church rejects it. For example, John Paul II writes:

By acknowledging and teaching the existence of intrinsic evil in given human acts, the Church remains faithful to the integral truth about man; she thus respects and promotes man in his dignity and vocation. Consequently, she must reject the theories set forth above [consequentialism and proportionalism], which contradict this truth. (John Paul II 1993, 83)

Yet, what does proportionalism have to do with DER, which finds its home in an anti-consequentialist account featuring exceptionless moral norms? Why even address it in this work? Ironically, proportionalism originates in the thought of the Roman Catholic theologian Peter Knauer, who attempts to ground it in Aquinas's treatment of double effect. Knauer, in the seminal article of proportionalism, cites q.64 a.7 as the exemplar of proportionalistic thinking.[2] He pays particular attention to the following passage in that article: 'But some act arising from a good intention can be made unlawful if it is not proportionate to the end [*proportionatus fini*]. And so, if someone in defending his own life uses greater violence than is necessary, it will be unlawful. But if he moderately repels violence, it will be a lawful defense' (Knauer 1967*a*, 133). One would think that by the phrases 'proportionate to the end' and 'moderately repels violence' Aquinas would mean, as Knauer himself suggests (not as an interpretation, but as his independent observation), that 'one may not kill an aggressor, however unjust, if in other ways one can save oneself and other possible victims' (ibid. 152). Similarly, this concept of an act's being proportioned to its end operates in Knauer's judgement that 'a physician may prescribe a drug which has bad side effects only until medical science finds a drug just as effective but without the side effects' (Knauer 1967*b*, 102). This criterion—that an act must be proportioned to its end—is not exotic. It is commonly understood that what should be done to attain an end is that which is requisite to effect the end. In the case considered by Thomas, the act by which the defender preserves his life while causing the least harm to the aggressor would be proportioned to the end of self-preservation.

Knauer, however, thinks that Thomas proposes something different from, though similar to, this principle of

---

[2] On the importance of Knauer's article, see Hoose (1987), 1.

moderation. He understands Aquinas to mean: 'In sinning, man seeks a real good, but his act in its total existential entirety is not proportioned to this good. Then the evil arising thereby, whether it is desired or not, belongs objectively to the act and is objectively what is "intended" ' (Knauer 1967*a*, 134). There are two significant problems with Knauer's account as an interpretation of Aquinas. First, he contradicts the statement with which Aquinas introduces his discussion of *proportionatus fini*. Thomas says that the act, even when it arises from a good intention (therefore, an act in which harm is not intended), may not be blameless if it is not proportioned to its end—in this case, self-preservation. Therefore, Aquinas holds that an act could originate from a good intention and not be proportioned to its end. Knauer denies this. Second, he maintains that Thomas, in his discussion of *proportionatus fini*, asserts that a harmful effect is intended if and only if the action productive of it causes less good than evil. Aquinas, however, distinguishes what the agent intends as an end from whether or not the act is proportioned to the intended end. Accordingly, he argues that the defender must not intend the death of the assailant and that the defender must not use greater force than is necessary to preserve his own life. According to Thomas, when the defender does not intend to take the life of the aggressor, but acts with excessive force, he would not act well, insofar as his use of force exceeds what is necessary for self-defence. Thus, Thomas excludes both the intentional taking of life and the use of excessive force. Knauer, however, holds that the act is an intentional taking of life when the agent uses excessive force.

Knauer attempts further to explicate Aquinas's account, saying 'Thomas also held that the evil might not be effected directly. According to him, the intention must be accidental (*per accidens*); it must be beyond intention (*praeter intentionem*)' (ibid. 136). Yet nowhere in q.64 a.7 does Aquinas speak of effecting the harm directly or indirectly, as Knauer claims. Moreover, Knauer asserts that Aquinas uses *praeter intentionem* to refer to an 'accidental' intention. Thomas, however, clearly denies that what is outside the intention is intended at all. Knauer describes what is not intended as intended in some special fashion. Thomas does not use the phrase, as Knauer maintains, to describe a way of intending.

Attempting to understand Aquinas's account, Knauer states:

There are further pairs of concepts which also stand in the same relation to the requirement of a commensurate reason. There are, for example, *per se–per accidens* and "in intention"–"beyond intention" in the text cited from St. Thomas [q.64 a.7]. The use of these different concepts for one and the same reality reveals that the scholastics had not reflected thoroughly enough on their meanings. (ibid. 139)

Knauer equates the distinctions *per se–per accidens* and *intentionem–praeter intentionem* with *proportionatus fini*, and defines the latter as 'having a commensurate reason'. In fact, as noted in section 1.1, Thomas holds that what is intended is essential in determining the goodness or badness of an act, while what is *praeter intentionem* does not have the same essential significance. He expresses this by saying that what is intended is *per se* and what is *praeter intentionem* is *per accidens* to the ethical analysis of an act. Because intention is essential to that analysis, Thomas argues that for a private individual's act of homicidal self-defence to be justified, the death of the aggressor must not be intended. Moreover, because the defender might gratuitously endanger the life of the assailant while not intending to take the aggressor's life, Thomas, as we saw in section 1.3, reiterates the criterion proposed by Pope Gregory IX (following Pope Innocent III, Ulpian, and Caius Cassius Longinus) that the force used in defence of life must be proportioned to the end of self-preservation.

Understanding his version of double effect to be the whole of morality, Knauer reduces the moral analysis of human action to his interpretation of what it means for an act to be proportioned to its end. With such whimsy, he founds proportionalism:

> I say that an evil effect is not 'directly intended' only if there is a 'commensurate ground' for its permission or causation. There are not two distinct requirements when I speak of the 'indirect causing' of evil and of 'a commensurate reason' for the act. The principle [of double effect] may be adequately formulated as follows: One may permit the evil effect of his act only if he has a commensurate reason for it. (ibid. 137)

While Aquinas distinguishes the intention of evil from any quantitative relation between the evil and good caused, Knauer maintains that an agent intends an evil effect if, and only if, the agent does not cause greater good than evil. Thus, if the agent were to cause greater good than evil by the act, the agent, according to Knauer, would not intend the evil. One could not more seriously misconstrue Aquinas or double effect.

To reiterate, by *proportionatus fini* Aquinas does not mean what Knauer asserts: that 'an objective is sought which has an appropriate price (*tantum–quantum*)' (ibid. 142). What would such a requirement amount to, if not a *quid pro quo*, a tit for tat, his life for mine? Rather, Aquinas proposes to denote a precondition for the use of such force as endangers the life of an attacker: the act of self-defence must be moderate. Thus, the use of a potentially lethal weapon is not to be countenanced when all that needs to be done is to turn on a light, or unleash the dog, or call for help, or throw a net or blanket over an attacker, even though the act of self-defence endangering the attacker's life would proceed from the good intention of self-preservation. The defender using force proportioned to the end of self-preservation does not hold the aggressor's life to be of lesser value than his own. Knauer's attempt to ground proportionalism on Aquinas's account of homicidal self-defence does not withstand scrutiny.

Knauer's account has another significant defect. As we have seen, he maintains that an agent intends a bad effect if and only if the agent does not cause more good than evil. When the agent effects greater good than evil, the agent does not intend the evil. For, Knauer holds, in such a case the agent has a commensurate reason for effecting the evil, namely, the good that he will bring about. As argued above, such a position cannot be attributed to Aquinas. Nor is such an account of the intention of evil tenable in its own right. The objects of intentions are ends and the means ordered towards those ends. Since means are discovered by deliberation, one intends them when one discovers them in deliberation and chooses them as ordered towards a given end. Accordingly, the question that arises when one asks whether or not something is intended by an agent is not: 'how much good did the agent realize by causing this thing?' Rather, one asks questions such as: 'did the agent's willing of the thing lead him to deliberate about how to achieve it?' and: 'was this thing done by the agent insofar as it was ordered towards the realization of some end the intention of which caused him to enter into deliberation?' Knauer, however, focuses exclusively on the quantitative relationship between the evil and the good effected by an agent. Thus, Knauer fails to account for the salient role of deliberation in determining what an agent intends and does not intend.

Moreover, he cannot account for our application of the concept of intention to ordinary cases in which one does not cause evil. By means of double-effect reasoning, we analyse exceptional cases in which we cannot realize a good end without also causing a bad effect. Nonetheless, the concept of intention by which we illuminate such situations is not limited to those circumstances. We examine such cases by employing the concept of intention which we acquire from ordinary cases, independently of our analysis of extraordinary cases in which the causing of good and evil are conjoined. Knauer, however, relies on an account of intention that is necessarily limited to cases in which both good and evil are effected. Thus, he lacks the resources to explain what it usually means for an agent to intend some object.

Although proportionalism began with Knauer, it did not end with him. Richard McCormick, who has been described as 'the champion of proportionalism' (Hoose 1987, 4), denies Knauer's account of the intention of evil. McCormick (correctly) thinks that Knauer renders the concept of intention vacuous, insofar as he makes the intention of evil depend on one's not causing greater good than evil. He amends Knauer's basic position by asserting that, for a great enough good, evil may be done intentionally (McCormick 1973, 94). McCormick thus makes proportionalism less ambiguously consequentialist and more clearly opposed to both Aquinas's account and double effect more generally.[3]

2.2.   ANTI-CONSEQUENTIALIST DEONTOLOGICAL ALTERNATIVES TO DER

While anti-consequentialist deontologists acknowledge the need for a casuistry of hard cases, not all agree that DER correctly resolves those it faces. I turn now to consider two alternatives.

2.2.1.   Donagan's casuistry of material guilt

In *The Theory of Morality*, Alan Donagan thinks DER amounts to the position that 'what lies outside the scope of a man's intentions in acting does not belong to his action, and so is not subject to moral judgement' (Donagan 1977, 164).

---

[3] For the intriguing history of proportionalism, see Hoose (1987) and Kaczor (2002).

Because he thinks it relies on the denial of responsibility for what one causes with foresight but without intent, Donagan rejects DER. DER, however, does not rely on such a position. Indeed, if one held that an agent who acts with foresight but without intent of a consequence lacked responsibility for that effect, the third criterion comparing the good and bad outcomes (present in all discernible versions of DER) would be otiose. It is not. DER holds agents fully responsible for what they cause with foresight but without intent.

In any case, realizing that his own deontological account requires something akin to DER to address hard cases, he presents a casuistry in which he defines murder as, 'killing another rational being who is materially innocent' (Donagan 1985, 875). Donagan contrasts material innocence with material guilt. He defines an agent's material guilt as, 'roughly, that what he is doing, even if his doing it is not voluntary, either threatens grave harm to himself or others or prevents himself or others from doing what it is their duty to do' (ibid. 883). He employs the terminology of material guilt to contrast physical acts attributable to an agent with the agent's mental states, which mental states comprise what we may call formal guilt. In keeping with Donagan's usage, one defines formal guilt as the agent's beliefs, desires, and intents to threaten unjustified grave harm. Of course, so defined, material and formal guilt do not exclude one another. An agent can be both materially and formally guilty.[4] In fact, common

---

[4] As noted in the Introduction, I prefer to speak in terms of material responsibility and formal responsibility in contrast to guilt. For I understand the term guilt to indicate blame. That is, the agent is not simply responsible; he is responsible for something wrong or unjust.

morality and law typically consider an agent guilty when he satisfies the criteria comprising both material and formal guilt. That is, the agent must unjustly physically threaten (be materially guilty) and mean to do so (be formally guilty). For Donagan, however, the category relevant to determining whether a killing is justified (in a hard case) no longer incorporates mental elements (such as the agent's beliefs, intentions, and so on), as formal guilt does. Rather, Donagan holds that one may justifiably kill the materially guilty, even when they are not formally guilty. With these terminological preliminaries in place, consider Donagan's account as applied to specific difficult cases.

One of the cases at issue is that in which, due to cephalo-pelvic disproportion, a baby cannot exit from the birth canal during labour (the earlier-noted craniotomy case). The baby will die, the mother will die, or both will die. Referring to Maimonides's position that the child may be treated as an unjust pursuer, Donagan holds that the baby may justifiably be killed as one materially (not formally) guilty of threatening the other's life. This concerns the subject of the norm prohibiting killing. Donagan thinks that, even though the baby cannot be described as acting, it may be killed. For 'a man is entitled to return the fire of a hunter who, thinking him to be a deer, innocently shoots at him, if only so can he save himself; and on the same ground he may kill somebody who strictly speaking is not acting at all, for example a berserk or drugged assailant' (Donagan 1977, 162). To be an unjust aggressor in the sense in which he uses the term (following Maimonides), one need not be doing anything at all. Indeed, applying this concept to a baby, one need not even be capable of responsible action.

Addressing the hysterectomy case, Donagan says that the foetus is an 'involuntary squatter; and as such it is not materially innocent' (Donagan 1985, 884). Since Donagan acknowledges that the foetus cannot be spoken of as doing anything, one wonders why he speaks of it as an involuntary squatter. It does nothing voluntarily nor involuntarily; moreover, unlike a squatter, the foetus belongs *in utero*.

Finally, Donagan considers the classic case of non-combatants in war. He says:

the deaths of noncombatants who are killed in direct attacks on military installations are to be deemed accidental, on the ground that it is the enemy's fault that non-combatants are there. Accordingly, in a just war, it is accounted permissible... to bombard installations even when it will result in the deaths of noncombatants. What is forbidden is directly to attack noncombatants or nonmilitary installations. (Donagan 1977, 87)

With respect to material guilt, however, Donagan does not indicate how he could justify the non-combatants's deaths. Presumably, the non-combatants lack even material guilt insofar as they threaten in no way. Indeed, he regards their deaths as primarily the responsibility of the enemy. Perhaps holding this, he does not think it necessary for those who would bomb to justify the harm they cause to the non-combatants. Yet, that the enemy has responsibility for the presence of the non-combatants nearby the military installation does not exonerate the bomber. For he voluntarily bombs knowing that the non-combatants will be killed.

Considering their deaths accidental conduces neither to clarity nor moral responsibility. Moreover, Donagan here appears to rely on the very concept of intent that he rejects. For how ought one understand, 'direct attacks' or 'directly to attack', if not as implying intent to attack? Again, does Donagan speak of the noncombatant deaths as 'accidental' in part because the tactical bomber does not intend them? It would appear that in dealing with tactical bombing, Donagan implicitly relies on the very concept (intent) he attempts to supplant.

Donagan's casuistry of permissible killing suffers from a number of deficiencies. First, material guilt, although applicable to human agents, is the wrong feature by which to justify killing. For (as noted in the Introduction) humans differ most markedly from other beings insofar as they are rational and, thereby, act voluntarily. One appropriately relates to another human when one attends to the presence or absence of voluntariness in his conduct. This, of course, requires attention to the mental elements of a human act, or to formal innocence and guilt. Formal innocence has ethical significance for inviolability, while formal guilt grounds justifications for killing a human. Second, Donagan uses material guilt in too metaphorical and labile a fashion to bear the weight of justifying homicide, the gravest harm we may cause another. Thus, one who cannot do anything becomes one who does things involuntarily and the foetus *in utero* becomes a squatter. Third, and finally, this casuistry erroneously indemnifies agents against responsibility for foreseen bad effects of their acts, as in the case of the tactical bomber who supposedly lacks responsibility for non-combatants's deaths. Donagan's account will not do. I now turn to another anti-consequentialist deontological replacement offered for DER, that to be found in the work of Frances M. Kamm.

2.2.2.   Kamm's principle of permissible harm

F. M. Kamm proposes a non-absolutist anti-consequentialist Principle of Permissible Harm (PPH).[5] While Kamm sympathizes with DER's prohibition against intentional harming, given her intuitions concerning certain cases, she finds DER too permissive in some respects and too restrictive in others. Kamm criticizes DER as too permissive insofar as she holds that DER would permit one to perform surgery on five patients knowing that by doing so one will kill a patient in an adjoining room as a side effect. In the case Kamm considers, the life-saving surgery on five patients releases a poison gas that kills one in the adjoining room.[6] Kamm rejects the permissibility of so acting, based on her intuitions. In this she agrees with Phillippa Foot, who first mooted the case (Foot 1978). In place of the too-permissive DER, Kamm proposes the Principle of Permissible Harm, PPH.

[5] Kamm proposes two versions, PPH1 and PPH2: (1996), 172–204. For purposes of comparing them to DER, the differences between the two versions lack relevance.

[6] I ask the reader's indulgence in entertaining the fantastic case Kamm entertains. One might change it to make it more faithful to that with which the world confronts one, but thereby lose Kamm's account. For example, as one reader more realistically suggests, one might encounter bacteria that survive the sterilization of surgical instruments such that one in five surgical patients contract a life-threatening infection.

The basic idea of PPH is that it is permissible for greater good *itself* to produce lesser harm. PPH rules out both 'lesser harm that is the side effect of mere means to greater good and the lesser harm that is brought about in order that greater good comes about (*one* type of case in which the harm is itself a means to the greater good)' (Kamm 1996, 184, original emphasis). DER and PPH both rule out the latter case of harming as a means to the greater good. For double effect does not permit an agent to intend the harm as a means to the good. Thus, DER and PPH differ with respect to lesser harm that is a side-effect of means to the good. That is, DER permits while PPH does not permit one to cause harm as a side-effect of one's means to the good. Kamm asserts that PPH would not allow one to perform surgery on five patients when the surgery (a mere means) results in a gas that kills the patient in the adjoining room. Kamm thinks, however, that PPH allows one to perform an operation that leads the five patients to breathe in such a way that they will disturb the air-flow and thereby cause poisonous gas to leak into a sixth patient's room. For it is not the operation (the mere means to the greater good) that causes the patient's death (the lesser evil). Rather, it is the five patients being alive (and breathing in a certain way because of the operation) that cause the patient's death. For Kamm, this has ethical relevance. Why? Because, according to her, when the greater good itself causes the lesser evil, one weighs moral status against moral status. That is, one compares the moral status of five patients to the moral status of one. In contrast, following Kamm's way of imagining the case, DER permits one to weigh the operation (the mere means to the greater good) against the patient's life. The operation, how-ever, lacks, while the patient possesses, moral status. According to Kamm, one illegitimately compares something lacking moral status to something possessing it. Yet, one reasonably asks, why think that one weighs the operation against the patient's life at all? Is it not more realistic to think that one compares the lives of the five patients as they require the operation to the life threatened by the very same operation? Moreover, if in virtue of one's moral status one may cause lesser harm, why may not the means neces-sary to one's continued existence cause comparable lesser harm? This disagreement concerns not how we should think about these hard cases, but how we should imagine them in our mind's eye. I, for one, do not see a path to resolve such idiosyncratic differences. There is, however, a more substan-tial criticism to be made of Kamm's account. That concerns the Principle of Secondary Permissibility, or PSP, with which Kamm complements PPH.

With PSP Kamm asserts that when PPH justifies some lesser harm and one can minimize that harm by an act that would otherwise be impermissible, one may so act. For example, if PPH permits one to bomb tactically thereby killing non-combatants, then when one can reduce the harm to the non-combatants by terror bombing them, one may terror bomb. Basically, PSP says that when causing lesser harm is permissible in terms of PPH, then consequentialist considerations permit causing even less harm even when doing so is not permissible considered independently of the PPH-justification. PSP remains anti-consequentialist while incorporating consequentialist considerations. It does so lexicographically, by requiring PPH to be satisfied prior to PSP coming into play.

PSP significantly alters, however, the notion of moral status in virtue of which one resorts to PPH in the first place. For the moral status in virtue of which one may not permissibly terror bomb (at the primary level addressed by PPH) appears to go by the wayside in PSP. Kamm herself convincingly argues that the moral status of a person is such that any one violation of a person's moral status lowers the moral status of all persons (Kamm 1996, 279–80). Thus, when one may prevent another five murders by committing one, it makes sense not to commit the one. For one ought not to murder because it violates the moral status of all sharing in that status and not solely the moral status of the one murdered. Yet, PSP clearly violates the moral status of the non-combatant victims in virtue of which one resorts to PPH in the first place. In short, in Kamm's position the commitment to the inviolability of persons that leads one to adopt PPH profoundly opposes the harm-reduction strategy that recommends PSP. This incompatibility has greater significance than the above-noted differences concerning how one imagines hard cases. Moreover, even if Kamm were to reconcile the internal inconsistency between the moral status of persons required by PPH with PSP, PSP remains unacceptable. For it radically undermines personal inviolability in virtue of which one resorts to a casuistry of hard cases in the first place. In hard-case justifications one reveals the limits of norms while sustaining their exception-less character. Kamm fails to do so.

As noted earlier in discussing the poisonous-gas case, Kamm rejects DER in part for being too permissive. She also thinks that DER is too restrictive. She has in mind a set of scenarios modelled on what she calls the munitions-grief-case. I now consider such cases and her criticism of DER as too restrictive. In the munitions-grief-case, a bomber seeks to destroy the munitions plant knowing that it will be rebuilt by the local citizens unless their children are also killed. The children's deaths will so devastate the parents that they will be unable to rebuild the plant. As it turns out, if the bomber destroys the plant, the children will be killed. For they play at a nearby school. Knowing this, the bomber destroys the plant and kills the children. Kamm holds (cor-rectly) that as an intentional terrorizing of the children DER does not permit this act. Employing PPH, however, Kamm judges it permissible. For the greater good (the plant's destruction) causes the lesser evil (the children's deaths). With respect to the question of the intent of the bomber, Kamm holds that he bombs because it will kill the children, but not in order to kill the children. She asserts, 'the PPH distinguishes, within the class of seeming intentional harms, between acting *in order* to harm and acting *because* there will be harm' (Kamm 1996, 184, original emphasis). What does Kamm distinguish in differentiating between acting in order to harm and acting because there will be harm? Consider a tactical bomber who knows that a forest has been destroyed and that, were this not the case, his bombing of the munitions plant would be in vain, for the lumber necessary to rebuild it would be readily available.[7] The fact that the forest has been destroyed explains the bomber's act, as a given, background condition. In this sense, he bombs because. He does not bomb in order to destroy the forest (indeed, given his knowledge of its destruction, he cannot rationally do so). Here, acting because clearly differs from acting in order to. One must change the case, however, to resemble Kamm's munitions-grief-case. In such an instance, the bomber knows that the factory would be rebuilt if the forest were not destroyed. Yet, he need do no more than bomb the plant, for this will destroy the forest also. Knowing this, he drops the bombs, destroying the factory and the forest. In this second case, how ought one describe the tactical bomber's dispositions vis-à-vis the destruction of the forest? As will be noted in section 3.4.3, intended means characteristically enter into practical deliberation as solutions to problems posed by one's intended end. The tactical bomber seeks to destroy the plant and chooses bombs, a bombing path, and so on, to do so. He also seeks that the plant not be rebuilt, but he need not choose any further means to achieve this. For what he intends as means to destroy the plant also ensures that it will not be rebuilt. Thus, the end of not having the plant rebuilt, while it does pose a problem to him in practical deliberation (he needs to solve the question of how to achieve it), does not require anything more of him than dropping the bombs. To discern

[7] I owe this and the following example to a conversation with Professor Jorge Garcia.

intent in cases in which an agent need do nothing in addition to what he has already chosen to do, one need ask whether the agent regards the destruction of the forest as something he succeeds in doing and, thereby, intends. (I address the relation between intent and success in section 3.4.4.) Considering such questions, may we reasonably say that the pilot bombs because, but not in order to destroy the forest? No. For the destruction of the forest now stands in the foreground of his act, in part defining his act as a success. It no longer acts as a background condition (because); rather, it acts as one that the bomber himself seeks (in order to), even though he does nothing more than he would already do. Nonetheless, he regards it as an achievement; he successfully destroys the forest. Therefore, one does not correctly describe his bombing as done because, but not in order to destroy the forest. If one gives moral weight to the i/f distinction (as Kamm does in cases in which the intended greater good itself causes the lesser foreseen evil), then DER rightly prohibits the munitions-grief-case.

To sum up, Kamm's account depends upon idiosyncratic intuitions, cannot incorporate PSP without thereby undermining the inviolability of persons and the relevance of PPH, and fails to distinguish acting in order to from acting because. As an alternative to DER, Kamm's account leaves much to be desired. Thus far, I have considered proportionalism as a consequentialist declination from DER and anticonsequentialist deontological alternatives such as Donagan's casuistry of material guilt and Kamm's PPH. Finding these deficient, I now turn to prominent contemporary versions of double effect.

2.3. CONTEMPORARY VERSIONS OF DER

In the 1960s (largely through the work of Elizabeth Anscombe—for example, her *Intention* of 1957 and her classic essay 'Modern Moral Philosophy' of 1958—coupled with the rise of applied ethics, particularly medical ethics) DER entered the mainstream of contemporary Anglo-American ethics and moral psychology. Contemporary thinkers have attempted to articulate the grounds for employing this approach to hard cases. Separately, Warren Quinn and the trio of John Finnis, Germain Grisez, and Joseph Boyle offer accounts of double effect. I now consider these contemporary versions.

2.3.1. Warren Quinn's account

As will be addressed more thoroughly in section 4.3, DER depends upon the ethical relevance of the i/f distinction. In his account, Warren Quinn locates the distinction's ethical relevance in the specific way in which those harmed as a means enter into the agent's thinking. He argues:

[An agent intending harm as a means] has something in mind for his victims—he proposes to involve them in some circumstances that will be useful to him precisely because it involves them. He sees them as material to be strategically shaped or framed by his agency. Someone who harms by direct agency must therefore take up a distinctive attitude toward his victims. He must treat them as if they were then and there *for* his purposes. But indirect harming [in which the agent foresees but does not intend the harm] is different. Those who simply stand unwillingly to be harmed by a strategy—those who will be incidentally rather than usefully affected—are not viewed strategically at all and therefore not treated as for the agent's purposes rather than their own. (Quinn 1989, 348, original emphasis)

Quinn finds the objectionable character of intending harm as a means in the attitude the agent necessarily takes toward those harmed. He says, 'what seems specifically amiss in relations of [intending harm as a means] is the particular way in which victims enter into an agent's strategic thinking ... as material to be strategically shaped or framed by his agency' (ibid. 348). Call this the user-attitude. Quinn understands acts executed with intentions formed in deliberations imbued by the user-attitude to be impermissible. This way of thinking about the victims (as matter to be shaped, as existing for the sake of the agent's goals) infuses such acts with its own morally objectionable character. Accordingly, other things being equal, an act instantiating the user-attitude requires greater justification than one free of that defect. With the user-attitude, Quinn successfully articulates one crucial aspect of DER. There are, however, telling problems with Quinn's account.

In her magisterial *Intention*, Elizabeth Anscombe argues that an agent's acceptance of the question, 'why did you do ——?' when asked in reference to what happens when he does something indicates that what happens is intentional under the description the question offers (Anscombe 1957). The question does not have a special meaning. What is unique is that to which one applies the question. The agent knows both this and its cause without observation. For example, while one knows without observation that one's eye twitches, one does not know without observation why one's eye twitches, unless one twitches one's eye. That is, there is the solely neurological twitching of one's eye (the cause of which is not known without inspection) and the actress's twitching of her eye (without investigation, the actress knows she causes her eye to twitch). Following Anscombe, the intentional differs from the foreseen as effects and their causes that one knows without investigation differ from those known with observation.

With this contrast in mind, if we ask our neighbour why he cuts the grass and he responds, 'in order to spruce up the yard', while when we ask him why he sweats he says, 'oh, yes, I did not notice. It cannot be helped; it goes with sprucing things up', then he distinguishes an intended from a foreseen consequence. He intentionally cuts the grass and spruces things up; he does not intentionally sweat. He may foresee that he will sweat, but he does not accept the application of the question in the relevant sense. If to our question about his sweating he had replied, 'in order to lose weight', then his sweating would be intended.[8]

Quinn notes that Anscombe offers a straightforward account of intention that has the resources to discriminate a foreseen from an intended consequence. Nonetheless, he thinks that there is a difficulty with this account when applied to the standard double-effect cases. He asks:

[8] Note that the contrast is not between what can and cannot be known without observation. Rather, one distinguishes how the agent does know the matter in question.

What if the agents in the problematic cases... become philosophically sophisticated? Perhaps they will then come to reject the
'why' questions in the manner of their counterparts. The terror
bomber, for example, might respond by saying, 'The actual deaths
can't be helped if I am to create the realistic appearance of death
and destruction.' By giving such answers he and the others will be
opting for a more demanding criterion of the intentional. (Quinn
1989, 340)

Quinn thinks that agents could reject Anscombe's question
and begin to understand their intentions so that only that
which immediately contributes to their ends would be intended. Quinn offers this as a more demanding criterion for
accounts of DER. He thinks that, insofar as it relies on the i/f
distinction, DER ought to be tenable on any plausible theory
of the intentional. So, he thinks that the opponents of DER
ought to be given the greatest latitude in paring their intentions down to 'their indisputably intentional cores' (ibid.
341). However, as Anscombe notes (Anscombe 1957, 47)
one asks the philosophically sophisticated agents 'with what
intention do they pare their intentions?' Paring intentions
admits application of the intention-referring question.
Quinn does not acknowledge that this question renders
the paring of intentions vacuous. In any case, I now consider
the account he offers conceding (the suspect) paring of
intentions which I will address at greater length in 3.3.1.

Facing the paring of intentions, Quinn argues that to
determine whether an action involves solely a foreseeing or
an intending is to ask whether the one harmed is an object of
an intention. He asserts:

[DER] distinguishes between agency in which harm comes to some victims, at least in part, from the agent's deliberately involving them in something in order to further his purpose precisely by way of their being so involved (agency in which they figure as *intentional objects*) [direct agency] and harmful agency in which either nothing is in that way intended for the victims or what is so intended does not contribute to their harm [indirect agency]. (Quinn 1989, 343, original emphasis)

Applying this direct agency/indirect agency construal of the i/f distinction to the craniotomy and hysterectomy cases, we see that in craniotomy the foetus figures as an intentional object. For it is precisely by its head being crushed that the doctor furthers his purpose of saving the mother's life. In hysterectomy, however, the foetus is not an intentional object. For neither the removal of the foetus from the mother's body nor the death of the foetus furthers the preservation of the woman's life which purpose the hysterectomy advances. Quinn accepts the doctor's claim that the death of the foetus is not intended. The foetus does figure as an object of an intention in craniotomy while it does not in hysterectomy. In terror and tactical bombing, the same holds.

Considering the usually contrasted cases of terminal sedation/euthanasia, Quinn acknowledges that there is no such asymmetry. In both cases the patient figures as an intentional object, and it is precisely insofar as the patient so figures in the doctor's action that the patient's death comes about. In terminal sedation, the pain of the patient is to be relieved precisely by her receiving the barbiturate drip. In euthanasia, the patient's pain is to be ended by the lethal drug. Thus, Quinn does not capture the i/f distinction in all of the standard cases. He acknowledges this, but does not consider this inability to account for all of the standard cases to be a decisive point against his account. He thinks that advocates misapply DER to what he calls non-conflict situations in which the relevant goods of individuals do not conflict. He maintains, 'if stopping pain is urgent enough from the patient's perspective to make death acceptable as a side effect, it ought to make death acceptable as a means' (ibid. 343, n. 17). Quinn acknowledges that in the usually contrasted cases of terminal sedation/euthanasia the patient figures as an intentional object. He does not see this as problematic. For he considers the proper purview of DER to be inter-, not intra-personal. So understood, DER comes into play only in cases of harm to others.

Fischer, Ravizza, and Copp think that Quinn's account not only does not (as Quinn admits) include the pain-relief case on the side of indirect agency, but that he includes too much on the side of direct agency. They argue:

[Quinn's account] would, e.g., classify a military commander's orders in a justified war as direct agency. (We owe this sort of example to Kenneth Kemp.) Suppose that such a military commander orders his troops into battle in a certain way, as a result of which some of the soldiers die. Here, the commander has deliberately involved his soldiers in something in order to further his purpose precisely by way of their being so involved; further, harm comes to them as a result of this. But, presumably, the commander's ordering his troops into battle in wartime is not a violation of their moral rights. (Fischer *et al.* 1993, 710, n. 8)

This appears to be a significant problem for Quinn. The troops are intentional objects, the harm comes from their involvement, and the commander furthers his purposes precisely by their being so involved. Yet, prima facie, this case should be classified as an instance of foreseeing, not as an instance of intending harm. So Quinn's account captures too much in the case of the commander.

This problem concerns Quinn's qualification, 'precisely by way of their being so involved'. In order to make sense of this phrase it is necessary to investigate the agent's intention. The commander's intent determines the precise way in which he involves the soldiers. Consider King David and Uriah. This was a killing and not simply a commander's deployment of a soldier because of the intention in accordance with which David sent the Hittite soldier to fight; namely, in order to effect his death.

Quinn's precise way cannot be cashed out without analysing the content of intention. Yet, Quinn aspires to agnosticism with respect to this very matter. For he hopes to offer an account of the i/f distinction that functions even when agents pare their intentions to the bare bones, as it were. That is, the point of the account is to function solely on the basis of an agent's having an intention without further scrutinizing that intention. Thus, unobjectionable cases such as Kemp's commander appear to pose a problem for Quinn.

Quinn, however, can overcome the objection posed by Kemp. For Quinn gives intent no intrinsic ethical import. Rather, he proposes that intent has relevance only insofar as persons have rights that incorporate reference to intent.[9] Quinn holds that the presence of a right not to be used or

---

[9] On this point see McMahan (1994), 201.

harmed without one's consent activates the badness of the intentional non-consensual harmful using of another. According to Quinn, the wrongness of direct agency does not reside in the agent's intent. Rather, one locates this wrongness in the victim's right not to be so used.[10] Reconsidering Kemp's commander, since the soldiers do not have a right not to be so used by the general, Quinn's account does not rule out sending them into battle. While Quinn can respond to Kemp's criticism, his account significantly departs from DER in which intent has intrinsic ethical relevance. In place of DER, Quinn would present a catalogue of certain rights, some of which refer to intent and thereby occasionally parallel DER. Of course, this coincidence of judgements does not make Quinn's account an instance of DER. Moreover, as noted, Quinn's account of intention-referring-rights does not capture DER's evaluations in terminal sedation and euthanasia. Let us now entertain one final contemporary account of DER.

2.3.2. Finnis, Grisez, and Boyle's account

John Finnis, Germain Grisez, and Joseph Boyle have, individually and as a group, published work on DER that

---

[10] In my arguments for the ethical relevance of the i/f distinction, I argue both that intent has relevance in itself (at sec. 4.3.1) and that the status of persons articulated as ends and not means thereby incorporates reference to intent (at sec. 4.3.2). My account of the latter Kantian aspect of the ethical import of the i/f distinction differs from Quinn's insofar as he refers to rights while I understand the moral status of persons itself to exclude intentional misuse or victimization. Moreover, following Kant, one may not intentionally victimize oneself; DER is both inter- and intra-personal, contra Quinn.

stretches over the past three decades. In what follows, I consider the trio's articulation of DER. Most recently, Finnis, Grisez, and Boyle hold that, 'in morally evaluating human actions, one must identify the action to be evaluated from that perspective [of the acting person] rather than from the perspective of an observer' (Finnis *et al.* 2001, 12). In their account, the perspective of the acting person enjoys a certain privilege when it comes to describing an action and the intentions constitutive of it. For example, they say, 'the truth about what is intended and being done is available, primarily if not exclusively to the acting person *in* that acting—*in* that deliberating, choosing, and carrying out the choice—which constitutes the reality to which all accounts of intention and action must conform if they are to be true' (ibid. 34, original emphasis). These authors hold that agents enjoy privileged access to their own minds and intentions.[11] They assert, 'though observers can often infer in some respects the morally objective descriptions of another's act, his or her proposal never can be an observable object' (ibid. 33). Certainly (as I argue in section 3.4.4) when an agent acts, an agent knows what he does. This, however, does not mean that others do not know what the agent does. For a crucial resource in terms of which an agent knows what he does is language. This he shares with those who observe what he does. So, for example, a soccer player who scores a goal relies on the same language to describe what he does as those who observe him. While he may at times more confidently know why he does it, he has no

---

[11] Anscombe (1957) argues cogently against such a (Cartesian) account.

special access to what he does. Because both agents and observers share language and employ it to deliberate about, intend, do, and describe actions, their perspectives do not differ as Finnis, Grisez, and Boyle propose. Of course, an agent may correct how others describe his act. To use Anscombe's memorable example, when I open the curtain and thereby focus light in your eyes, causing you to say, 'stop doing that!', I may deny the appropriateness of describing my act as a focusing of light in your eyes. I do so by noting that I did not know I was doing that. Finding this plausible, you accept my description of what I do and do not do. Similarly, observers may correct how an agent describes his act, noting that we do not use language as the agent proposes. Remembering that the South African prime minister Dr. Verwoerd said that he would 'really describe *apartheid* as good neighbourliness', D'Arcy notes that observers may reject an agent's description (D'Arcy 1963, 18). (Or, as Alice says to Humpty Dumpty, ' "glory" does not mean "a nice knock-down argument" '.) In short, neither the agent nor the observer's perspectives enjoy privilege when it comes to describing actions. Rather, it is in terms of a shared language that all speak plausibly or implausibly of what agents do.

Turning to their consideration of craniotomy, Finnis, Grisez, and Boyle say, 'a surgeon who performed a craniotomy and could soundly analyze the action, resisting the undue influence of physical and causal factors that would dominate the perception of observers, could rightly say "No way do I intend to kill the baby" and "It is no part of my purpose to kill the baby"' (Finnis *et al.* 2001, 24). Again, these authors hold that, 'in craniotomy done for the purpose of saving at least the mother's life, the object of the act [what the agent intends as a means] is to reduce the size of the baby's head so that the baby or its corpse can be removed from the birth canal' (ibid. 25). In a craniotomy, the physician cuts the baby's skull, removes its contents, destroys the skull by tearing it apart, and then removes the corpse from the birth canal. An observer would plausibly think that the physician kills the baby in order to preserve the mother's life. Yet, according to these authors, the physician need not intend the baby's death. For the physician need not propose killing the baby as his means of preserving the mother's life. He may propose to reduce the size of the baby's head. May the physician plausibly speak, however, using the terms of the medical vocabulary and common language, of reducing the size of the baby's head? No. Simply put, there is no such procedure. This contrasts with the hysterectomy of a gravid uterus, in which a physician without violence to medical or ordinary language performs a hysterectomy and speaks of doing so.[12]

Finnis, Grisez, and Boyle find ordinary language too restrictive for DER. In its place they propose conceptual necessity (treated more fully in section 3.3.3). H. L. A. Hart considers such an account, saying, '[a] foreseen but unwanted outcome will be taken to be intended if it is of a kind so immediately and invariably connected with the kind of action done that the connection is regarded as conceptual

[12] For an allied approach regarding the hysterectomy and craniotomy cases with respect to their relations to medical practice, see Flannery (2001), 185.

rather than contingent' (Hart 1967, 12). Following this line
of reasoning, one violates the norm against killing the innocent when one cannot help but conceptualize one's act as
killing. Moreover, in order to violate a norm against intentionally killing the innocent, the agent would have to conceptualize the act as a killing of the *innocent*. (Note, too, that
these thinkers construe the norm against killing so narrowly
that one does not violate the norm against killing when one
intentionally grievously harms.) According to this criterion,
if the very meaning of what one proposes to do is to kill,
then one intends to kill. Consider, for example, the meaning
of 'assassinate' and 'execute' in contrast to 'decapitate' and
'dismember'. When one assassinates or executes, one kills by
conceptual necessity. When one decapitates or dismembers,
one kills and does so with necessity, but by causal, not by
conceptual necessity. That is, when one intends to execute
one conceptually intends to kill. For killing is part of the
very concept. However, on this account, when one intends
to decapitate one need not intend to kill. For killing is not
part of the very definition of what one proposes (although
death is causally necessary).[13] With such an account, Finnis,
Grisez, and Boyle hold that the physician in the craniotomy
case may intend to decapitate the baby without thereby
intending to kill it. One wonders what this account prohibits. For it would seem to rule out few killings as violating the

---

[13] One notes, however, that the concept 'human being' correctly understood may be such that to decapitate a human being is, conceptually, to kill
the human being. Or, for that matter, to cut off the head of any living thing
that has one is, conceptually, to kill that living thing. I will not develop these
points further. Here, for the sake of argument, I entertain the position that to
decapitate is not conceptually to kill.

exceptionless norm against killing the innocent except those
in which death conceptually constituted what one set out to
do. (Again, the victim being innocent must also figure in the
proposal. Moreover, as noted, this construal of the norm
against killing does not prohibit intending profound harm
that falls short of death.) The authors note that a craniotomy, although not a violation of the exceptionless norm (so
understood) still may be unjust. They say:

> even if a craniotomy can be done without violating the command-
> ment and moral norm that exceptionlessly excludes intentional
> killing, isn't it unfair to the baby and as such wrongful, and
> therefore homicidal? We do not consider that question in this
> paper, since it is not settled by what the acting person intends as
> an end or chooses as a means. (Finnis *et al.* 2001, 25, note 37)

Here, the relevant issue now becomes the justice of non-
intentional killings of the innocent, in contrast to whether
one intends to kill the innocent. Thus, the question is not
whether one has violated the norm. Rather, it concerns
whether one acted unjustly towards the innocent. Yet, such
a construal of double effect renders it no longer capable of
definitively addressing the permissibility of one's act in a
hard case. If these authors are correct, one's act may be
justified by double effect, yet not permissible. This profoundly changes the function of DER as sufficient to determine permissibility in the relevant hard cases. To the extent
to which Finnis, Grisez, and Boyle depart from the way
in which agents use language and understand the norm
against killing, their account proves linguistically implausible and practically insufficient as an answer concerning the

permissibility of hard cases. Moreover, their account requires DER to be complemented by other considerations to determine the permissibility of acting in a hard case.

In light of the preceding criticisms of the most prominent alternatives, revisions, and accounts of DER, I turn to the more positive task of presenting a tenable form of double effect faithful to ordinary language and the norms that lead one to have recourse to double effect in the first place.

3

The i/f distinction: distinguishing intent from foresight

The i/f ('intended/foreseen') distinction plays a crucial role in DER by differentiating an agent's intention of a harmful means from his foresight of a harmful concomitant of his means or end. I now offer characteristics in terms of which one distinguishes intent—of ends and means—from foresight of concomitants. I address the differences in terms of which one distinguishes intent from foresight, focusing on both the intention of an end and the intention of a means. In DER, controversy surrounds three issues (going from the least- to the most-disputed). First, whether one can differentiate intended means from foreseen but not intended causally necessitated consequences. Second, whether one can apply this to the contrasted cases as is typically done in DER. Third, whether this has ethical relevance. In section 3.4 I argue that one can distinguish intent from foresight; in section 3.5 I apply the distinction to the classically contrasted cases, arguing that DER correctly parses the intended from the foreseen. That is, that in the cases of euthanasia/terminal sedation, craniotomy/hysterectomy, and terror bombing/tactical bombing, DER rightly classifies the first member of each pair as intentional harming and the second as foreseen and not intentional harming. In section 4.3 I will argue for the ethical significance of the distinction.

3.1.   COMING TO TERMS

I speak of the i/f distinction. This naming of the distinction at issue in double effect is not standard. For reasons that will become evident, it ought to become so. Sanford Levy notes that the distinction receives a variety of names:

> There is significant terminological variation amongst proponents of [DER]. . . . I spoke of the distinction between directly and indirectly willing evil, but others speak of the distinctions between directly and indirectly intending, intending and permitting, the intended and the unintended, doing and allowing, direct and indirect voluntareity and direct and indirect action. Within the context of [DER] all these refer to the distinction between means and ends on the one hand and side effects on the other. . . (Levy 1986, 30)

I now consider these ways of speaking and indicate the preferability of 'intended/foreseen'.

3.1.1.   'Side effects'

As Levy notes, the referents of the first part of the distinction are intended objects, that is, means and ends. For this reason it is worthwhile using 'intended' to denote the first part of the distinction. For this is precisely what means and ends share: being intended. Since the referent of the second half of the distinction is a side effect, it could be named the 'intended/side effect' distinction. The advantage of 'foreseen' over 'side effect' is evident in this: presumably, not all side effects are foreseen. Therefore, to denote something as a 'side effect' remains ambiguous as to whether or not it is foreseen. Moreover, the distinction applies to the agent's relation to the consequences of the action. 'Foreseen' aptly indicates that the agent knows or believes something about the side effect. So, on the face of things, 'intended/foreseen' captures the referents of the distinction. 'Intended' refers to ends and means while 'foreseen' refers to side effects; all three (ends, means, and side effects) relate to the agent and, thereby, have ethical significance.

Often, proponents of DER speak of the foreseen effect as being merely foreseen, or only foreseen. The problem with this practice is that these terms carry with them the connotation of lesser import: that somehow a consequence merely foreseen is not that bad to effect. One best avoids this rhetoric in articulations of the i/f distinction. If one finds it necessary to emphasize the point, 'solely' nicely indicates that the foreseen effect is not intended.

3.1.2. 'Direct' and 'indirect'

'Direct' and 'indirect', while employed frequently, mislead opponents as well as advocates of DER. Levy notes that proponents of DER apply these terms to willing, intending, voluntareity, and action. He himself chooses to call the distinction one between 'directly and indirectly willing'. Additionally, and most unhappily, the terms refer to how one causes a consequence, as in the following passage: 'other evils also may be indirectly effected, but depending on the circumstances they are permissible even when intended directly. For example, physical pain may be directly caused for a sufficient reason' (Walsh and McQueen 1993, 364). The authors of this passage use 'direct' and 'indirect' ambivalently to refer to both causing and intending. This confuses the issue. For while in a given case agency may not be direct in the sense that proponents of DER attempt to capture (intended), causality might be direct (immediate) and vice versa. Thus, an agent can intentionally achieve some end in an indirect (mediated) fashion and directly (immediately) effect some consequence not intended. 'Direct' and 'indirect' modify agency and causality. Again, this confuses. For what is at issue in the distinction is not a contrast between what one causes (or allows) as an agent and what one causes (or allows) simply, but a contrast found within one's agency—a contrast between what one causes (or allows) with intent and what one causes (or allows) with foresight without intent.

To illustrate: one causes another's pleasure by whistling whether one does so with knowledge or in ignorance and whether one does so by coercion or without coercion. If one knows that one does so and one does so without coercion, then one voluntarily causes another's enjoyment: her enjoyment is attributable to one as an agent, not only as a cause.

So, when I walk down the street whistling pleasantly to express happiness, I voluntarily cause pleasure to others. One can also intentionally cause pleasure. Of course, intending to cause another's pleasure is voluntary; the point is it is more than voluntary. Say a street performer seeks a few coins and deliberates about how to make money by entertaining others and chooses to do so by playing the violin. The street performer would cause pleasure to bypassers intentionally while I would do so voluntarily, but not intentionally (for I do not seek to cause them pleasure, but knowingly do so). The i/f distinction contrasts the intentional from the voluntary (as I argue at greater length in section 4.3.1). As I have here argued, it does not contrast (as the terms 'direct' and 'indirect' imply) either what one does as an agent with what one does simply as a cause, or different ways of causing (immediately or mediately).

Moreover, those who use 'direct' and 'indirect' sometimes explain what they mean entirely in terms of what is intended or foreseen. So, for example:

In general terms, direct killing occurs when a person's death, by act or omission, is intended, whether as an end in itself or as a means to another goal. Indirect killing occurs when the death is not so intended, but is, rather, a foreseen consequence of some action or omission aimed at an end other than the death of the person. (Walsh and McQueen 1993, 358)

In fact, 'intended' and 'foreseen' are less general, more specific terms than 'direct' and 'indirect'. It serves no purpose further to characterize the intended as direct and the foreseen as indirect. As Anscombe notes, ' "direct" and "indirect" are dodgy terms; sometimes they relate to off-shoots, as it were, from a given sequence of causes, and sometimes to immediacy or remoteness, and sometimes to what is intended or not' (Anscombe 1982, 22). Dodgy terms have no role in DER.

3.1.3.   'Permitting', 'allowing', and 'accepting'

Another common way of speaking of the foreseen effect noted by Levy is to speak of it as allowed, permitted, or accepted. What about these ways of speaking? The following quotations illustrate the all-too-common use of 'allowed' and allied terms:

The agent intends only the good effect. The bad effect can be foreseen, tolerated, and permitted, but it must not be intended. (Beauchamp and Childress 1994, 207)

The distinction between what we intend and what we merely allow to happen. (Fried 1978, 23)

The agent may not positively will the bad effect but may merely permit it. (Connell 1967, 1021)

Not, however, as intended but only as permitted ... (O'Donnell 1991, 27)

One acts in a still different way in so far as one *voluntarily accepts side-effects* caused incidentally to acting. (Finnis *et al.* 1987, 289, original emphasis)

A permitted side-effect ... (Devine 1974, 45)

Yet, in the typical cases of double effect does the agent allow, permit, or accept the harm as opposed to causing it? Do 'permit', 'allow', and 'accept' express the agent's relation to the foreseen effect? No.

To say that an agent permits, accepts, or allows some effect grounds two inferences. First, that some cause other than the agent brings about the effect. Second, that the agent could but does not prevent the effect from coming about by intervening. For example, when I allow a leaf within my reach to flow downstream, some cause other than I carries it downstream—the current—and I could but do not prevent it from going downstream. Yet, in the standard cases to which DER receives frequent application (the death of a terminally ill patient due to sedation and non-combatant deaths due to tactical bombing) the agent cannot be said to accept, permit, or allow the foreseen bad effects. In these cases the need for DER arises from the ethically troublesome aspect of the agent's voluntarily causing harm. Consider tactical bombing. The bomber does not allow the deaths of the non-combatants by his non-intervention in an independent causal process. Rather, he drops bombs on or nearby them. He thereby causes their deaths. He kills them. When used as universally applicable to cases of double effect 'allow', 'permit', and 'accept' are worse than unhappy.[1] This is not to say that the

---

[1] Philippa Foot notes the inaccuracy of using 'permitting' of the foreseen harm: 'it is interesting that the disputants [in DER] tend to argue about whether we are to be held responsible for what we allow as we are for what we do. Yet it is not obvious that this is what they should be discussing, since the distinction between what one does and what one allows to happen is not the same as that between direct and oblique intention. To see this one has only to consider that it is possible deliberately to allow something to happen, aiming at it either for its own sake or as part of one's plan for obtaining something else' (Foot 1978, 25). Among those whom she takes to conflate the two

distinction between intending and foreseeing does not apply
to a permitting or an allowing. Indeed, as Nagel notes, 'it is
also possible to *foresee* that one's action's will cause or fail to
prevent a harm that one does not *intend* to bring about or
permit .... (One point worth stressing: the constraints
apply to intentionally *permitting* as well as to intentionally
doing harm ...)' (Nagel 1979, 130, original emphases).
Nonetheless, while one can foreseeably permit something,
to foresee is not to permit, as contrasting 'intend' with
'permit', 'allow', and 'accept' implies.

3.1.4. 'Unintentional' *or* 'unintended'

Some speak of the foreseen effect as being unintentional or
unintended.[2] Treating these terms as synonymous, what do
they imply? Of course, both may mean what one does not
intend. For this reason they come to mind when one attempts to contrast the intended with what is foreseen but
not intended. Ambiguity attends the terms, however. For, as
John Finnis notes, ' "unintentionally" connotes accident or

distinctions is Bennett in his 1966 article. In that article, perhaps misled by
advocates of DER, Bennett tends to treat DER as either equivalent to, or as
presupposing the relevance of the doing/allowing distinction. He misses
Foot's point that the i/f distinction applies to doings and allowings. For a
discussion of Bennett's 1966 article, see Casey (1971). In more recent work on
double effect, Bennett (1995) notes the difference between the do/allow and
intend/foresee distinctions while not acknowledging the moral relevance of
either.

   [2] The following, among others, speak of the intended/unintended distinction: Coughlan (1990), 58; Beabout (1989), 49; Khatchadourian (1988), 25,
n. 6; and Marquis (1978), 28. Cooney (1989), 201 speaks of the 'desired/
unintended' distinction.

mistake or lack of foresight' (Finnis 1991, 48). This connotation makes 'unintentional' particularly unfit for use in
DER where one foresees the harmful effect.

Moreover, 'unintentional' is not the contradictory of 'intended'. For 'unintended' denotes both intending-not-to-x
and not-intending-to-x.[3] The contradictory of intending-to-
x is not-intending-to-x, *not* intending-not-to-x.[4] Accordingly, it is best not to characterize the foreseen effect as
being unintentional. For the point is that the foreseen effect
is not intended. The distinction does not differentiate what
one intends to effect from what one intends not to effect. If
one intends an end insofar as one attempts to realize it
through those things ordered to its achievement (means),
then one who foresees that he will cause x by y-ing cannot be
said to intend not to effect x unless he takes means not to
effect x. If a submariner foresees that he will definitely kill

[3] I owe this point to my reading of D'Arcy (1963).

[4] Presupposing rationality, an agent who intends to x does not also intend
not to x. Thus, agents who intend, for example, to terrorize, cannot intend
not to terrorize. Similarly, an agent who does not intend to x cannot intend
not to x while foreseeing x as a causally necessary result of his intentionally
doing y. For example, a tactical bomber who foresees that non-combatant
deaths result necessarily from bombing cannot intend not to kill non-combatants. (Of course, this does not mean that he intends to kill non-combatants.) I understand this position to be the more difficult for DER. If it were
possible for an agent who foresees x as an inevitable result of his intentionally
doing y and who does not intend to x, also to intend not to x, then it would be
possible for the agent who foresees and does not intend that harm will result
from his act to intend that it not result. If a person intends that harm not
result from his act, then he acts benevolently. Acting benevolently would
positively recommend what he does. So, for example, the tactical bomber,
unlike the terror bomber, could intend not to kill the non-combatants. As
mentioned, I do not think that this is possible in cases where the tactical
bomber foresees their deaths as resulting with necessity.

some submariners in a flooding submarine by closing a door, then, although in intending to preserve the submarine, his own life, and the lives of other submariners he need not intend to kill the crew members in the flooding section, he cannot thereby claim to intend not to kill those submariners.

In light of the above considerations, one most precisely characterizes the distinction operative in DER as the intended/foreseen distinction where one understands the foreseen as not intended. One notes, however, one caveat. As I argue in section 4.3.1, one does not find the ethical relevance of the i/f distinction in an ethically important difference between volitional and epistemic states (as intended/foreseen might imply). Rather, one—at least partially—locates that ethical import in an agent's different volitional dispositions towards consequentially comparable states of affairs.

Having come to terms, I now turn to the more substantive consideration of how to distinguish intent from foresight in cases of double effect. I first consider the problem facing the distinction, then methods proposed to distinguish intent from foresight, and finally, present my own account.

3.2. THE PROBLEM OF CLOSENESS

Philippa Foot moots the problem of closeness in her discussion of the now famous spelunker case. In this case (meant to illuminate problems thought to be less clear in the craniotomy case), a party of cave explorers face certain death if they do not remove a particular obstacle in their way, namely, a fat member of their party. Foot asks:

suppose that the trapped explorers were to argue that the death of the fat man might be taken as a merely foreseen consequence of the act of blowing him up. ('We didn't want to kill him ... only to blow him into small pieces' or even '... only to blast him out of the cave.') I believe that those who use the doctrine of the double effect would rightly reject such a suggestion, though they will, of course, have considerable difficulty in explaining where the line is to be drawn. What is to be the criterion of 'closeness' if we say that anything very close to what we are literally aiming at counts as if part of our aim? (Foot 1978, 21–2)

The i/f distinction exerts some of the negative force of DER. That is, it rules out certain actions as involving intended harm. In trying to understand how this could work, Foot proposes that in the justified cases the harm is more removed from what the agent does than in the cases not justified by DER. This way of maintaining the i/f distinction holds that in the cases in which the bad effect is thought to be intended, the harm is too close to what the agent does. The problem is to present a philosophically appealing criterion in terms of which both permissive and prohibitive aspects of DER function.

Turning to cases, how can one plausibly claim in the removal of a cancerous gravid uterus, for example, that the agent foresees but does not intend the non-viable foetus's death that results with causal necessity? Moreover, how can one hold this while claiming that in an obstetric craniotomy the agent intends the foetus's death as a necessary means to the preservation of the mother's life? Foot proposes that one might initially answer this question by noting the proximity between the craniotomy and the baby's death and by contrasting this to the distance between the hysterectomy and the foetus's death. Yet, what criterion could demarcate the two outcomes from their associated acts? Of course, advocates of DER aspire to propose something more definite than the spatial metaphor of closeness. They do so in order to differentiate the intention of a means from the foresight of a causally necessary effect of what one intends.

3.3. RESPONSES TO THE PROBLEM OF CLOSENESS

Before considering proposed criteria, I wish to articulate more precisely the claim that DER makes. I do so for two reasons. First, to avoid one possible misunderstanding. Second, to clarify what a successful response to the problem of closeness would (and would not) establish. I hope to avoid being misunderstood as saying that it is simply impossible for an agent in a double-effect case to intend the harmful effect. An instance of this misunderstanding would be, for example, if one were to think that DER's proponents claim that a physician cannot intend to kill a patient by administering a barbiturate drip. DER proponents do not hold this.[5]

---

[5] Indeed, given the legality of administering a barbiturate drip for the purpose of relieving pain, if one did intend to kill a terminally ill patient, one way of doing so covertly would be to sedate him with barbiturates and claim palliation as one's intent. I do not advocate this; I do note that the clinical act called terminal sedation admits of various intents. The crucial point for DER is that amongst these intents is that of relieving pain while foreseeing but not intending death. When this intent is present, one properly speaks of terminal sedation. On a related point, see the following note.

In accordance with DER, one proposes that an agent who, for example, voluntarily terminally sedates, tactically bombs, or surgically removes a gravid uterus *can but need not* intend the harm attending those acts. That is, it is possible but not necessary to intend harm in these cases.[6] Moreover, DER maintains that an agent who voluntarily terror bombs, performs a craniotomy, or euthanizes cannot fail to intend terror, killing, maiming; the death of or grievous harm to the foetus; or the patient's death.[7] As Anscombe notes, an agent cannot deny that he intends the means to an intended end (Anscombe 1957, 44). The point is analytical. DER holds that an agent in a permissible case can truthfully claim to foresee but not intend harm while an agent in the impermissible cases cannot. For in the latter cases, unlike the former, the agent intends harm as a means to an end. It is, therefore, necessarily intended. A successful response to the problem of closeness will contrast the necessarily intended with the possibly but not necessarily intended (the foreseen). I now look at attempts to do this before offering an account of intention by which one distinguishes intent from foresight in the debated cases.

---

[6] If the agent did intend harm, say, in the tactical-bombing case, then since intent defines one's act (as I argue in sec. 3.4.4) one would redefine that act—perhaps as tactical-*cum*-terror bombing.

[7] That the agent acts voluntarily excludes cases, for example, of ignorantly dropping bombs on a civilian population or removing an uterus one does not realize is gravid.

3.3.1. Directing, paring, or withholding one's intention

Could double effect rest upon a direction of one's intention away from what one foresees one will inevitably cause? As noted in section 1.1, the infamous Jesuitical *grande methode de diriger l'intention* is a non-starter. For any paring or shaving of intentions itself is an intentional act and runs up against the question proposed by Elizabeth Anscombe: with what intention does an agent pare his intentions? She argues:

> Is there ever a place for an interior act of intention? I suppose that the man I imagined, who said 'I was only doing my usual job', might find this formula and administer it to himself in the present tense at some stage of his activities. However, if he does this, we notice that the question immediately arises: with what intention does he do it? This question would always arise about anything which was deliberately performed as an 'act of intending'. (ibid. 47)

Thus, paring or shaving does not eliminate intent. Rather, they both indicate intentions regarding intentions (or, second-order intentions). Pascal mordantly satirizes an interior act of intention while Anscombe offers a decisive philosophical objection to any double-effect account that relies on the directing, paring, or withholding of intentions. Certainly, an agent can direct, pare, or withhold his intentions. Indeed, intentions bearing on intentions, like beliefs about beliefs (for example, the belief that some of our beliefs are true), merit attention in exhaustive discussions of intent. DER, however, cannot repose soundly upon a method that would have us count a second-order intention as itself not being significant. For, if intentions possess moral relevance, one would plausibly think that second-order intentions do also. In short, the direction of intention is a non-starter as a way of differentiating intent from foresight.

3.3.2. The counter-factual test

In attempting to distinguish between solely foreseeing an effect and intending means and ends, some employ the counter-factual test. Charles Fried formulates the test as follows:

There is a traditional criterion for distinguishing an intended means from an unintended but foreseen concomitant, the counter-factual test: if the morally relevant result at issue... could somehow miraculously be prevented and events thereafter allowed to take their natural course, would the actor still have chosen to act as he did? (Fried 1978, 23)

Fried alludes to a case in which a man, seeking to free his friend from prison, explodes a charge knowing that it will free his friend as well as kill a guard.[8] If we apply the test, what do we learn when the man answers, 'yes' (that he would explode the charge if the guard were not killed and his friend were freed from prison)? Does this response, as

---

[8] The scenario appears to be based on the famous Victorian case in English law: *R. v. Desmond, Barrett, and Others*. Kenny describes this case: '[a] Fenian conspirator was found guilty of murder because, by dynamiting the wall of Clerkenwell prison to liberate two imprisoned fellow-conspirators, he had caused the death of persons living near-by' (Kenny 1973, 145). In secs. 4.3.3 and 5.6 I consider the moral and legal relevance of foresight of a concomitant of an otherwise wrongful act.

supposed by advocates of the test, tell us that in the case in which the guard's death occurs, it is not intended? No. For the man might intend both to free his friend and to kill the guard. That he would explode the charge solely to free his friend does not warrant the conclusion that he would not explode it to kill the guard. The agent may have the conjoined intentions to free and to kill. Since his intention to free might suffice for him to act, his acting where the death of the guard will not occur does not tell us that in the case where the death and the freeing of his friend both occur, he does not intend to kill the guard. So, when the man tells us that he would explode the charge in order to free his friend even if the guard were not killed, the test tells us that he intends to free his friend, as stipulated.[9]

James Sterba notes that the test successfully determines: '(1) whether the action is an intended means to the good consequences; [and] (2) Whether the good consequences are an intended end of the action...' (Sterba 1992, 25). As he notes, however, the test cannot determine whether the evil consequences are foreseen, but not intended. Since disputants on each side agree that the agent intends a benefit, there is no need for the test. For it tells us what is not at issue; namely, that the agent intends the good effect. At issue is how to differentiate a foreseen concomitant from an

---

[9] If the man answers 'no' (maintaining that he would not explode the charge unless the guard were to be killed), while we may not thereby conclude that he does not intend to free his friend, we may conclude that he does intend to kill the guard. For such an answer agrees with only two possibilities: either the man intends to kill the guard and does not intend to free his friend; or he intends both to kill the guard and to free his friend and neither end alone suffices to move him to act.

intended outcome. The test does not serve.[10] It may point in a helpful direction, however.

As a complement to the test, Sterba proposes a non-explanation test. He says, 'according to this test, the relevant question is: Does the bringing about of the evil consequences help explain why the agent undertook the action as a means to the good consequences?' (ibid. 26) When the agent answers, 'no', Sterba argues that the agent foresees the evil consequences; when 'yes', the agent intends them. Sterba offers this test as tending to be the best way of resolving doubts concerning whether an agent intends or solely foresees an effect. This test has its merits. For example, in the case of a tactical bomber, the harm to the civilian population does not explain the action; in the case of administering a barbiturate drip for pain relief, the death does not explain the administration of the analgesic.

Expressed intentions characteristically explain intentional actions by answering the all-important questions of why and how the agent acts. The non-explanation test relies on an account of intention in which intentions explain actions. This is as it should be. Sterba notes the place to look in offering a test that relies upon the explanatory character of intention. In section 3.4, I articulate such an account. Before doing so, I entertain one last attempt to distinguish intent from foresight and thereby address the problem of closeness.

---

[10] Kamm understands DER to rely on the counter-factual test to distinguish the intended from the foreseen. Much of her criticism of DER can be met by noting the deficiency of the test (which she herself seems to consider a viable way of distinguishing intent from foresight: Kamm 1996, 181).

3.3.3.   Conceptual necessity

By definition, to assassinate or to execute is to kill (as noted in considering Finnis, Grisez, and Boyle's account at section 2.3.2). Therefore, to intend to assassinate or execute is to intend to kill. Similarly, to terror bomb is to terrorize by means of bombs that kill, maim, and destroy. Therefore, to intend to terror bomb is to intend terror, killing, maiming, and destruction. To perform an obstetric craniotomy is to cut a hole in a baby's cranium, remove its brain, and dismember its skull. Therefore, one who intends a craniotomy intends to remove the baby's brain and dismember its skull. Prima facie, to intend a craniotomy is to intend to kill the baby. Conceptually, however, to intend a craniotomy is not to intend to kill. For the definition of a craniotomy does not include killing the baby.

Conceptual necessity indisputably delimits what is too close to one's intent to be counted as foreseen. If one's intent conceptually includes the effect, then one intends that effect. Conceptual necessity analytically (and, therefore, most narrowly) establishes what one intends. All agree that one does intend the conceptually necessary effects of one's act. Nonetheless, few on either side of the debate think that conceptual analysis includes all of what agents intend (except, perhaps, Finnis, Grisez, and Boyle, as noted at section 2.3.2). One intends more than that included in a conceptual analysis of the words one employs to describe one's acts. An agent's expression of intent leads us to ask her why and how she plans to act, just as she herself has already addressed these very questions in her deliberations concerning the act of which she speaks to us. I now turn to these (why and how) questions to offer an account of intent that has room for the i/f distinction without being limited to it.

3.4. AN ACCOUNT OF INTENTION

In one discipline presupposed by ethics, intention stands at the centre. This more particular inquiry Elizabeth Anscombe, to whom the credit belongs for its revivification, calls moral psychology. In contemporary philosophy it has come to be called action theory. As the saying has it, 'action theory is where all the action is'. The following topic alone could form a book-sized study. Although I offer more than an *ad hoc* account of intention to found the i/f distinction and address the problem of closeness, I do so not by entering into all, or even many, of the mooted questions concerning intention. Rather, I note intention's distinguishing characteristics, in particular its relation to action, deliberation, and practical knowledge.[11] I will first consider how intentions differ from feelings, as some thinkers conflate the two in discussions of double effect.

3.4.1. Intention and feelings

Intentions concern objects apprehended as desirable. 'Desire', however, is ambiguous, as Finnis notes:

[11] As readers familiar with their work will note, I am indebted to my readings of Anscombe (1957) and Bratman (1987).

'[d]esire' (like 'want') is indeed equivocal... between (i) one's
response to an intelligible good *qua* intelligible and understood
to be good (whether or not morally good), i.e., *qua* rationally
motivating, and (ii) one's response to what, as a concrete and
experienced or otherwise imaginable possibility, appeals to one's
feelings;... One can choose and intend to do what is utterly
repugnant to one's dominant feelings—that is the important
reality (or the most important of the realities) which judges recall
when they state, at large, that one can intend what one does not
desire. (Finnis 1991, 35)

An intention concerns an object apprehended as rationally
motivating; that is, grasped as good to effect (or, *mutatis
mutandis*, to allow, a point addressed in section 5.2). What
one sees as good to effect, however, may strike one as
affectively unappealing. For example, I intend to get out of
bed early in the morning and, accordingly, set my alarm to
do so. I do not, however, eagerly look forward to, nor at the
time the alarm sounds will I feel like, getting out of a warm
bed. An intention differs from a feeling as a cause differs
from an effect and as one's action differs from one's reaction.
The former is an effective, causal desire; the latter, an affective, emotional response. Differing from feelings, for example, of regret or relief, intent may be allied with either.
This point bears on the i/f distinction insofar as the terror
bomber, for example, may abhor the non-combatants's
deaths while intending them. Conversely, an agent may
welcome some result he does not intend. In the terminal
sedation case, for example, the physician and family may be
relieved at the death that ends the patient's ordeal without
thereby having intended to kill the patient. Thus, intentions

differ from feelings. While this point removes one potential misunderstanding, more must be said concerning what an intention is and how it differs from foresight. I now turn to these tasks.

3.4.2. Intention as volitional commitment to a plan of action

Intention incorporates a volitional commitment to achieving what the agent grasps as good and realizable by his action. In this respect, intention differs from merely seeing something that one could do as good. As Bratman notes, 'intention involves a special commitment to action that ordinary desires do not' (Bratman 1987, 16). An agent's intention instantiates a volitional commitment not to be found in his mere desire for some object or grasp of something's goodness. The former does while the latter do not indicate the agent's possession of and commitment to a concrete plan of action. For intention is the agent's volitional commitment to achieving a goal by means of a plan of action.

The contrast reveals itself in the difference between saying 'I desire to go to Venice', and 'I intend to go to Venice'.[12] In wanting to go to Venice, I see it as a good that I may achieve. In intending to go to Venice, however, I have a plan to go to Venice to which I commit myself and in accordance with which I save money, reserve vacation time, arrange

---

[12] I here modify an example Bratman presents.

transportation, study Italian, and perform myriad other acts. As a plan to which I am committed, intention constrains me (rationally) from having other, incompatible intentions, and, thereby, from acting in ways inconsistent with my plan. For example, my plan of action restricts me from planning to go to Tokyo and from studying Japanese instead of Italian. Simply wanting to go to Venice does not implicate me in having a plan to do so. Nor does merely wanting to go to Venice for the month of May prevent me (rationally) from wanting to go elsewhere in May, say Tokyo. Thus, as a volitional commitment to achieve what one wants by means of a plan an intention differs from a mere want or desire.

As a plan of action, intention is something concrete, complex, formed, and—when it comes to fruition—executed. It is concrete, insofar as it unifies specific elements to form an aggregate; complex, as comprised of ends (both intermediate and ultimate in a given series) and means (some of which serve as intermediate ends); formed, as the result of the planning process called deliberation; and executed, as the action it informs follows it. Like any plan, it can be revised or abandoned as the volitional commitment vivifying it apprehends better ways of achieving the end or a more desirable goal.

Considering intention's plan-like character, recall Aquinas's discussion of intent (noted in section 1.1) in which he proposes that intention is the act of the will with respect to the end, 'as the term towards which something is ordained' (I-II q.12 a.1 ad 4). As a plan of action, intent has both a terminus and a way (the means) leading towards that end.

Employing Thomas's example, I will the end, health; choose the means, medicine; and intend the concrete, complex unity of end-through-means, health-by-means-of-medicine. One wills ends; chooses means to them; and intends both ends and the means ordered towards their achievement.

To intend health is to commit to a plan of action in accordance with which I achieve it, say, taking this heart-medicine. My intending cardiovascular health (and, thereby, overall health) by means of medicine leads me to see a cardiologist, secure a prescription, go to a pharmacy, and consume the medicine in certain amounts and at certain times. Contrast intending health by means of medicine with foresight that, as it so happens, certain things I consume because I enjoy them—for example, olive oil, garlic, and red wine—promote a healthy heart. This realization does not amount to a plan of action to eat and drink as a means to health. I do not follow my foresight or execute my action in terms of it. For example, foresight does not lead me to seek out the most healthful types of garlic and olive oil (those with the highest concentrations of beneficial properties). Nor does it constrain me to consume them in the amounts or at the times most conducive to health or indicate a volitional commitment to do so insofar as they are healthful. Moreover, I do not form and produce foresight by means of deliberation (a point developed in section 3.4.3). Rather, foresight is an awareness of causal relations. It is not, as an intention is, a plan of action one forms, commits to, and follows. (Of course, one could incorporate food and drink into a plan ordered towards health; merely knowing the causal relations between health and what one eats and drinks does not amount to such a plan.)

Similar points hold when the foreseen outcome is detrimental to health. For example, it amounts to a medical truism to note that medicine has undesirable side effects, ranging from the mere irksomeness of being drowsy to the gravity of organ-damage. Say that I know that the heart-medicine, for example, will adversely affect my liver. I do not commit to taking the medicine in terms of its harmfulness to my liver. I do not take measures to render my liver more susceptible to the damage I foresee (as I would were I to intend and, thereby, be committed to it). Indeed, foresight does not constrain me from acting to reduce the damage, for example, to refrain from drinking alcohol which would compound the harm. Of course, I cannot entirely eradicate the damage as it inevitably accompanies my taking of the medicine. Nonetheless, the foresight of liver damage caused by the medicine does not amount to a plan to which I commit myself in order to achieve this effect by this cause, as does my taking of the medicine ordered towards my health.[13]

Importantly, when I take the medicine in spite of knowing its harmful properties, foresight does indicate my volitional disposition towards the damage. Namely, I would rather

[13] Nagel alludes to the plan-like character of intent in contrast to foresight, in terms of how intent guides one, saying, 'action intentionally aimed at a goal is *guided* by that goal. Whether the goal is an end in itself or only a means, action aimed at it must follow it and be prepared to adjust its pursuit if deflected by altered circumstances. Whereas an act that merely *produces* an effect does not *follow* it, is not *guided* by it, even if the effect is foreseen' (Nagel 1980, 132, original emphases).

incur the harm to my liver than forgo the benefit to my heart and overall health. Moreover, just as my intent to take the medicine for the sake of health excludes (rationally) an intention not to take the medicine, so also my foresight that taking the medicine inevitably results in harm to my liver excludes the intention of avoiding this harm. (The moral relevance of foresight of a bad effect both involving a volitional disposition towards harm and excluding intent to avoid harm receives treatment in section 4.3.1).

Intention is an agent's volitional commitment to effecting a goal as planned. Foresight is a cognitive realization of what will occur given certain causal relations. Intent differs from foresight as a volitional commitment to a plan of action that takes advantage of certain causal relations to effect a goal differs from knowledge of causal relations.

As noted, we *form* an intention. Deliberation names the process by which we do so. Accordingly, one consideration in an account of intention concerns the steps leading to a fully formed intention. For an intention remains inchoate and partial until the agent discovers, chooses, and intends the means for effecting the end. This is the role of deliberation in the full formation of an intention. A consideration of deliberation reveals further grounds for the i/f distinction.

3.4.3. Intention and deliberation

As Aquinas notes, to intend is to tend towards. Tending towards involves a space through which the tending occurs. In intention, the analogue to the space intervening between the one intending and the object tended towards is the means, the by which, the *via*. Since to intend an end is to will it as achievable by some means, the question arises: how do agents discover means? There is a role for an act of reason that inquires into the means available for causing an end: deliberation.

The intention of an end answers the question 'why', while posing the problem 'how'. By deliberation the agent attempts to solve the problem 'how'. Bratman highlights this aspect of intention:

My theory of intention supports the commonsense distinction between intending some means and merely expecting some side effect. To see why, recall [the] roles of intention... Two of these roles concern the relation between future-directed intentions and further practical reasoning... These are the roles of intention in posing problems for further reasoning and in constraining other intentions. (Bratman 1987, 141)

As a plan of action to which the agent is volitionally committed, intention constrains further intentions, and, thereby, further acts informed by intent (as noted in section 3.4.2). Moreover, intention supplies the question of deliberation (or, in Bratman's phrase, poses a problem for further reasoning): how can I bring about this intended end? The intention of an end leads an agent to deliberate about effective means. When successful, deliberation completes the formation of the (thus far, partial) intention by discovering means. When the agent still intends the end, and deliberation succeeds, the agent intends and chooses the means effecting the end. The intention now has the complete form, end x by means y.

Typically, many means stand between the end intended and the agent's realization of the end. These means themselves serve as intermediate ends relative to other means. (As noted in section 3.4.2, this point bears out the complexity of intent as a plan of action.) One drives the car to get to the party, one fills the tank to drive the car, one pays the attendant to fill the tank, one opens one's wallet to pay the attendant, and so on. Characteristically, the intention of the end (the final in a series) issues in deliberation concerning means which, in turn being intended, lead to further deliberation, serving as intermediate ends relative to other means, and so on.

As Bratman notes, that intention (both of the final end in a series and intermediate ends—which may also be referred to as intended means) issues in deliberation distinguishes it from a belief such as foresight (ibid. 125). A foreseen effect may be considered in deliberation; as foreseen, however, it does not cause deliberation. (Of course, as the example of foreseeing the healthful effects of certain foods indicates, foresight coupled with desire to achieve health may become a commitment to a plan of action to eat these foods which in turn leads to deliberation about, for example, where to buy the most healthful types.) Intention characteristically issues in deliberation because it poses the problem that deliberation solves: how do I achieve this? That intention characteristically does while the foresight of an effect characteristically does not cause deliberation (by posing problems of how to achieve an outcome) distinguishes intent from foresight.

This point holds even when means discovered by deliberation effect a foreseen outcome. Means effect the foreseen result as a cause, not insofar as they are means. For as means they are more than a cause. Namely, they are a cause used by an agent. 'Means' denotes a governing agency not denoted by 'cause'. Means relate to the intended end through the agent's deliberation. In deliberating, the agent attempts to discover what cause will bring about a particular effect. That effect as intended is the end; the cause as intended is the means. Thus, agents intend and choose means based upon their causal properties vis-à-vis an intended effect—an end. Means may cause a number of effects; they are means, however, only to the extent to which an agent intends that which they effect. So, for example, in billiards the cue ball may hit the eight ball and cause it to go in the side-pocket. As thus described, there is a causal relationship between the cue ball and the pocketed eight ball. If a player deliberates about hitting the eight ball into the side-pocket by using the cue ball, then the relation of cue ball to pocketed eight ball is one of means to end. Such a relation subsumes that of cause to effect. To reiterate, unlike foresight, intention causes deliberation insofar as it poses the question deliberation attempts to answer: how do I achieve this end (intermediate or final in this series)?

Two affiliated features of intention that further delimit it from foresight relate deliberation and further intentions concerning means. As noted, the intention of an end characteristically causes deliberation concerning means.

Similarly, the intention of an end conjoined with successful deliberation concerning means results in the choice and intention of those means best answering deliberation's question. Thus, intentions concerning ends cause (*via* deliberation) further intentions concerning means, the intention of which solves deliberation's problem of how to effect an intended end. These differences further ground the i/f distinction. For foresight of an outcome does not cause one to have other intentions, bearing on that outcome, or, for that matter, upon any effect whatsoever. Nor does foresight answer deliberation's question of how to achieve a goal. (Rather, when it is a foreseen bad effect, such as harm to the liver attending heart-medication, it only further complicates matters.)

Thus, intention and foresight differ in terms of their relationship to deliberation. Intentions characteristically: (1) cause deliberation; (2) issue in further intentions through deliberation; and (3) (as further intentions) solve deliberation's problem. Foresight does not characteristically relate to deliberation in these signal ways. I now attend to one final, often neglected, characteristic of intentions. Anscombe draws attention to this feature of the knowledge operative in action; namely, intentions as practical knowledge.

3.4.4. Intention as practical knowing

What happens when I do something differs from what I do. Anscombe notes that I know my act without observation while I know what happens only by observation (Anscombe

1957, 13–20). Accordingly, when you ask me what I do I can tell you straightaway, without looking. Using Anscombe's example, opening a window, letting fresh air into the room, and focusing sunlight in your eyes, I am drawn up short by your saying 'stop doing that!' When I say 'stop doing what?' I do not feign ignorance. Without observation, I know my act of opening the window and freshening the room. Without observation, I do not know that my act involves the focusing of light in your eyes because I do not intend to focus light in your eyes. Anscombe proposes that my intending is my knowing my act without observation. This is practical, in contrast to speculative knowledge. Anscombe argues that intentions indicate the peculiar nature of practical knowledge to be a knowing that causes what it knows. This knowing contrasts with knowledge caused by what it knows. For example, running a marathon, a jogger finds out and subsequently knows that she sweats. From her knowledge one cannot infer that she intends to sweat. She knows that she runs without observation; she observes that while she runs, she sweats. If the runner were to reply to our question 'why do you sweat?' by answering 'I noticed that I was sweating, I guess it comes about from running the race', then such a response indicates that she sweats with foresight but without intent. If we ask her why she wears down her sneakers and soaks her jersey with sweat and, doing all of these things, she knows that she does them only by observation, then she knows these speculatively, not practically.[14]

---

[14] Anscombe denies that just anything can go into the foreseen, not intended category. As noted in discussing the problem of closeness in sec.

In other words, practical and speculative knowledge differ in terms of their directions of fit. Directions of fit relate the world and the mind as standards measuring one another. The world may judge the mind or vice versa. In speculative knowing the mind does or does not conform to the world. Here we speak in terms of truth when the mind correctly relates to the world and of falsity when it does not. In contrast, in practical knowing the mind or agent's intent acts as the standard to which the world lives up or of which the world falls short. Here we speak of success and failure. Anscombe notes this difference with a memorable example—presented here with slight modifications (ibid. 56). Two men go to a grocery store. One has the task of filling his wife's list; the other, a detective, has the task of recording what the husband buys. For the husband the direction of fit goes from the list, representing his wife's mind, to the world. His wife's intent judges the world. Success (practical truth) is the cart being filled with the items on her list. For the detective, these relations reverse. The direction of fit goes from what the husband actually puts in his cart to the

3.3, she says that an agent cannot assert that means to an end acknowledged as intended are not intended. Presumably, if our runner were to say that she intends to win the race while she does not intend to run the race we would be justified in denying that she intended the end and not the means. When something is established as the means to be employed to achieve some end, then if the agent intends the end, the agent necessarily intends the means. So, although on Anscombe's account there is some flexibility for an agent to delineate what happens from what she does, there is not total plasticity. Moreover, intention is not the private domain of the agent in such a way as to render external assessment vacuous. In fact, as Anscombe maintains, when we want to know what a person intends, we usually need only cursorily look at what she does. This ability is a function of the nature of language as common.

detective's record. The world judges the detective's mind. In this case speculative truth (what we typically refer to as truth without qualification) is the detective's record matching the cart's contents. When the wife writes 'Romaine lettuce' and the husband buys iceberg, he cannot when she notes this—try as he may—correct the error by changing the list to read 'iceberg'. When the detective erroneously records a bottle of Zinfandel as 'Merlot', he can correct the error by erasing 'Merlot' and writing 'Zinfandel'. Thus, the directions of fit of speculative and practical knowledge differ and, thereby, the terms by which we evaluate them differ. To reiterate, we speak of the mind as true or false and of the world as a success or failure insofar as world and mind judge one another.

As noted, intent is practical while foresight is speculative knowledge. Accordingly, their directions of fit and respective evaluative terms differ. Intent defines what happens in the world as a success or failure while what happens in the world characterizes foresight as true or false. Consider the marathon-runner. Her intent to run the marathon defines her not finishing the marathon as a failure. If she were not to sweat, her foresight would be false; she would not, however, thereby fail. This point remains true even if from her not sweating one could conclude with certitude that she would not finish the race (perhaps one simply could not run that far without sweating). Thus, intention and foresight differ in terms of their directions of fit.

Finally, as a practical knowing (or, in other words, a making of an act in terms of intent), intent defines an agent's act and informs his actual physical performance; foresight does not. First, consider how intent defines one's act. It is a philosophical commonplace to note that intention differentiates acts from happenings. For example, my intention to blink my eye makes my eye's blinking an act in contrast to a happening (a mere twitching of nerves). So also, different intentions distinguish one act from another. Thus, my intent to blink my eye as a signal to you makes that act a signalling, whereas when I blink intending to get sand out of my eye, my act is a ridding my eye of an irritant. So, depending on intent, my act is defined as one of either signalling you or removing an irritant.

Consider also how intent informs the physical performance executed in terms of it such that if one's intent were to differ, one's physical conduct would also characteristically vary. When I intend to signal you, I face towards you; when I try to rid my eye of sand, I do not. Insofar as intent informs behaviour, the latter changes with intent.

In contrast to intent, foresight neither defines one's act nor informs one's conduct. Two otherwise similar acts that differ in terms of the agent's possessing or lacking foresight of some outcome need not vary in terms of their descriptions nor constitutive physical movements. For example, if the marathon-runner were not to foresee her sweating, the description of her act as *running a marathon* would not change. That is, her act is one of *running a marathon* regardless of her foresight of sweating or absence thereof. Also, her having or lacking foresight of the fact that she will sweat need not alter her physical behaviour as she runs the marathon. (Whereas, absent the intent to run a marathon, that physical behaviour partially constituting the running of a marathon would typically not occur.)[15]

Thus, intent names and typically determines what agents do; foresight does not. This does not mean that foresight lacks relevance in our assessment of responsibility. Nor does it mean that we do not include foresight in discussion of our act. Rather, it means that we name and perform acts primarily in terms of intent, not foresight. Accordingly, absence of or a change in foresight does not fundamentally alter act-description or typically change act-performance, while absence of or a change in intent does.

3.4.5. Salient differences between intent of a means and foresight of a necessary effect

The preceding discussion indicates the following prominent features of intention by which it differs from foresight. In terms of these characteristics, one makes the i/f distinction that differentiates an intended means from a foreseen effect

---

[15] Albeit not impossible, it would be odd (and a humorous Jacques Tati-like occurrence) to end up doing what marathon-runners do without the intent marathon-runners have. Some athletes do compete in what they refer to as 'centuries' or runs of 100 miles. In doing so, they run the course of over three marathons. Nonetheless, just as those who run a marathon do not run the 100-yard dash—although they run many 100-yard distances—so also those who run centuries do not thereby run three marathons, or even one, to the extent that doing so partially depends on one's intent, in terms of both defining one's act and determining one's physical conduct. On the latter point, note that the century-runners do not do what marathon-runners do; namely, stop after a certain distance. This is part of the behaviour that constitutes running a marathon.

causally necessitated by what one intends. First, due to its nature as a volitional commitment to a plan of action, an intention constrains action; foresight does not.[16] Second, intention characteristically causes both deliberation and further intentions; foresight does not. Third, the intention of a means solves deliberation's problem; foresight does not. Fourth, intent and foresight differ in terms of their directions of fit. As practical knowledge, intent defines an act as a success or failure; as speculative knowledge, foresight does not. Rather, what occurs characterizes foresight as true or false. Fifth, and finally, if one were to lack a specific intent, one's act could not be named by that intent and one's conduct typically would differ from what it would be were that intent present. However, if one were not to foresee some consequence of one's act, one's act would not need to be redescribed nor would one's behaviour typically differ.

In light of these and allied considerations, disputants in the debate concerning DER have come to acknowledge that intent differs from foresight. The more controverted question addresses the problem of closeness mooted in section 3.2. Again, that problem concerns how one may hold that agents necessarily intend harm in the impermissible cases while they need not in the permissible cases. How does one

---

[16] As noted in sec. 3.4.2 (in discussing the harm to one's liver caused by taking heart-medication), foresight of an inevitable consequence does prevent one from (rationally) intending and acting not to produce that inevitable effect. (Sec. 4.3.1 addresses the moral import of this point.) It does not, however, lead and guide one towards the production of that inevitable effect as a plan of action does.

apply the i/f distinction so as to parse the cases as DER does? Relying on the fruits of this account of intention, I now answer that question.

3.5.   APPLICATION TO CONTRASTED CASES

May one apply the preceding distinctions to the classic cases of DER: euthanasia/terminal sedation; craniotomy/hysterectomy; and terror/tactical bombing? As I now argue, according to the above-noted features of intention, these cases contrast as intended/foreseen instances of harming.

Consider the euthanasia/terminal sedation cases. In active voluntary euthanasia, the physician apprehends the cessation of the patient's pain as good or rationally motivating.[17] Being volitionally committed to this as his intended end, he deliberates about how to achieve it. In deliberation, he discovers that the way to end the patient's pain is to kill him. His intention to kill as a means of ending pain solves deliberation's problem of how to stop the pain. In turn, his intention to kill leads him to deliberate further concerning how to kill. For example, he seeks a painless, quick, perhaps even an economical means of killing. He finally decides and further intends to kill by injecting a specific lethal drug that

---

[17] In euthanasia, the patient's pain ends; it is not relieved. In order for there to be pain relief, the patient must exist. If, as in euthanasia, one ends the pain by ending the patient's existence, one cannot speak of relieving the patient's pain. Pain relief exists only when the subject relieved exists.

meets these criteria. The fully formed intention of ending the patient's pain by killing him with a lethal injection leads him to administer the drug. It constrains his action, by, for example, causing him to confirm that the dose is lethal. If he were to give the lethal injection and the patient's pain were to end without the patient dying, he would have failed in what he had set out to do. For he chose the lethal injection not only as a means to end the patient's pain, but also as a means to end the patient's pain by killing him. Of course, he would not have failed entirely, for his ultimate end was to end the patient's pain. Nonetheless, he would have failed to do this in the way he intended. Moreover, if he were to lack the intent to kill the patient (say he sought to treat an infection and did not know that he was giving a lethal injection) his act could not be correctly described as euthanasia.[18] In active voluntary euthanasia, the physician necessarily intends the death of the patient as a means to his intended end of pain-cessation. *Mutatis mutandis*, the same may be said for the patient who authorizes his own euthanasia.

In terminal sedation, the physician seeks to relieve the patient's pain and with this volitional commitment

[18] One notes that (as occurs in pharmacological errors in which physicians mistakenly kill their patients with lethal doses), absent the intent to kill the patient, one's conduct in administering the injection typically would change, but need not. The intent to administer an injection (of any drug) determines conduct so particularly that the absence of the intent to administer a lethal injection, while it does change one's act-description, it need not change one's performance. Of course, here the exception proves the rule. For the high degree of specification found in the intent to administer an injection causes little to change when one alters the drug one intends to administer.

deliberates about means to this end. Deliberation issues in the choice of a barbiturate-drip. He foresees that this will result in the patient's death with causal necessity (because, as stipulated, the barbiturate both deadens pain and suppresses respiration). Nonetheless, his foresight does not guide his action. For example, it does not lead him to ensure that enough barbiturate is present to suppress respiration. Unlike intent, his foresight does not cause him to deliberate about how to kill nor does it cause further intentions concerning means to kill. (As noted in section 3.4.2, in discussion of the heart-medicine that harms the liver, foresight does preclude him (rationally) from having the intention not to kill the patient.) Moreover, it does not solve the problem of how to relieve pain that he poses to himself in deliberation. Indeed, he may regard it as only adding to his deliberative problem and not solving it at all. If he were to administer the drip and the patient were not to die, his belief that she would die would prove false. Nonetheless, one may not say (solely referring to his falsified belief) that he would have failed in what he had set out to do. For one can speak of an act as a failure or a success only by reference to the agent's intent that establishes what success or failure would be. If he were to administer the barbiturate and not thereby relieve the patient's pain, he would fail. For this is what he intends. (This is so even if, from the fact that the patient did not die, one may conclude with certitude based on physiological necessity that the patient's pain was not relieved. For the patient's pain not being relieved counts as failure because of the doctor's intent.) Regarding how one speaks of what he does, if he had not foreseen that the barbiturate would also kill, he and others could still correctly describe what he does as sedation, or an act of relieving pain. One would not continue to call it terminal sedation, given the lack of foresight of the patient's death. This, of course, bears out the claim that the absence of intent unlike the lack of foresight requires a fundamental change in act-description. For the basic point of sedation is to relieve pain.[19] In terminal sedation, the physician need not intend the patient's death. That is, the act of putting a patient on a barbiturate drip admits of the intention of killing the patient, but it does not require that intention. (Again, *mutatis mutandis*, the same holds for the patient who requests terminal sedation.)

Thus, the euthanasia/terminal sedation cases contrast as necessarily-intended-death versus foreseen-not-necessarily-intended-death. They do so in part because the act of terminal sedation admits of a greater variety of intents vis-à-vis killing than the act of active euthanasia. Intentionally putting a patient on a barbiturate-drip corresponds with the intentions of relieving pain, of killing the patient, or both. Intentionally giving a patient a non-analgesic lethal injection (the exemplar of euthanasia) correlates with the intention to kill the patient or to end the patient's pain by killing him. That is, intentionally giving a patient a non-analgesic lethal injection implicates one in having the intention to kill while intentionally putting a patient on a lethal analgesic

[19] If he were to lack foresight of the lethality of the sedative, his conduct need not change. For foresight does not structure one's act as intent typically does. As noted, the specificity of administering an injection mutes this typical difference between intent and foresight in the euthanasia/terminal sedation cases.

need not. Clearly, the i/f distinction applies to euthanasia/ terminal sedation as DER proposes.

In the craniotomy/hysterectomy cases, both physicians regard the preservation of the mother's life as good or rationally motivating. Being committed to this goal, the physician in the craniotomy case deliberates about how to preserve her life, given the cephalo-pelvic disproportion. He decides to cut a hole in the baby's skull, remove its brain, crush its skull, and then remove its corpse from the birth canal. He intends to decapitate the baby, dismembering its skull piece by piece; in obstetrical terms, he does this when he performs a craniotomy. The doctor intends to behead the baby as the only way of saving the mother's life. Of course, while removing the baby's brain and dismembering its skull, he abhors and profoundly regrets his act and the tragic circumstances he understands as leaving him no other choice. Nevertheless (as argued when contrasting feelings from intent in section 3.4.1), he does intend to destroy the baby's head. The intent to dismember the baby's cranium directs his action. For example, it leads him to ensure that the surgical instruments he employs can cut and dismember the skull. If the physician were to use forceps that would not tear the baby's head apart, he would have to alter what he does in order to do what he intends. For he seeks to dismember the baby's skull. This intent causes him to deliberate about what surgical instruments to use and leads him to intend to use those deliberation discovers. The intent to destroy the baby's cranium solves the problem of how to preserve the mother's life. In terms of direction of fit, his intent defines his act as a success or failure. If he crushes the baby's skull and thereby preserves the mother's life, he succeeds in doing what he set out to do. If he were to fail to crush the baby's skull and the mother were to live, he would ultimately succeed and proximately fail to do what he had set out to do. He would succeed in saving the mother's life while failing to do so in the manner in which he had intended; namely, by crushing the baby's head. If he were to lack the intention to dismember the baby's cranium, his act would no longer properly be described as an obstetric craniotomy. Moreover, lacking that intent his conduct would differ.[20] For that intent partially defines and results in the conduct known as an obstetric craniotomy. In summation, in an obstetric craniotomy, the physician necessarily intends to destroy the baby's head. To do so is to intend grievous bodily harm to the baby.

In contrast, in the hysterectomy case the physician chooses to remove the cancerous, gravid uterus in order to preserve the mother's life, foreseeing that the non-viable baby will thereby die with causal necessity. This foresight prevents him from taking measures to preserve the baby's life. It does not, however, guide his act. For example, he does not, following this foresight, perform the hysterectomy in such a manner as to insure that the non-viable baby dies. Foresight does not cause him to deliberate about how to destroy the baby. Nor does foresight, as the intent to kill or grievously harm would, lead him to further intentions concerning, say, surgical instruments that would enable him to

[20] The intent to dismember the baby's skull so determines the surgeon's behaviour that no conduct in the vicinity of that which one performs in a craniotomy seems capable of being performed absent such an intent.

kill or gravely harm. The foetus's destruction does not solve his problem of how to preserve the mother's life; it answers none of his deliberative questions. In terms of direction of fit, if he were to remove the uterus and the baby were to live, his foresight would be false. He would not, however, thereby fail to achieve what he had set out to do in the manner in which he had set out to do it; namely, to preserve the mother's life by removing her cancerous uterus. Moreover, if he were not aware of the foetus, he could still perform the very operation he does perform, a therapeutic hysterectomy. His ignorance of the foreseeable consequence of the foetus's death need not alter how one describes what he does; nor need it alter the actual movements he makes.

In the craniotomy case the physician necessarily intends grave harm to the baby as a means of preserving the mother's life.[21] In the hysterectomy case, the doctor need not intend to kill or grievously to harm the non-viable baby. In sum, the i/f distinction applies to craniotomy/hysterectomy as DER proposes. I turn now to the final classic pair of cases, terror-/tactical bombing.

Consider terror and tactical bombing. Both bombers want victory as their good and commit themselves to its achievement, differing in terms of the means they adopt.

---

[21] A reader (reasonably) wonders why I do not simply state that the doctor kills the baby. Those who acknowledge the earlier noted conceptual distinction between decapitating and killing (found at secs. 3.3.3 and at 2.3.2 in discussion of Finnis, Grisez, and Boyle's account) may nevertheless find here a false and overly refined precision. I ask the reader's tolerance with respect to expression while drawing attention to the argument's conclusion. Namely, that the doctor in a craniotomy intends grievous harm to an innocent. Given the norm at issue, to so do is gravely wrong.

The terror bomber attempts to demoralize the enemy by killing, maiming, and, thereby, terrorizing non-combatants. The terror bomber necessarily intends harm to the non-combatants. Some find this conclusion questionable, asking why the terror bomber may not intend, for example, only that the civilians appear dead. This and similar intentions, however, pose specific deliberative questions; namely, how does the terror bomber intend to make them look dead? Of course, he can do so only insofar as dropping the bombs kills the non-combatants. For the civilians appear dead because they are dead. More importantly, the terror bomber achieves this goal by killing the non-combatants. Thus, the terror bomber requires the civilian deaths as a means to his intended end (even in the fanciful scenario in which he intends that they appear dead). He necessarily intends their deaths, maiming, and terror.

His action follows this intent. For example, it leads him to bomb when and, more importantly, because non-combatants are present. It causes him to deliberate about how to terror bomb. The intent to kill, maim, and thereby terrorize results in his intending the means of terror bombing. If some type of bomb were not to kill or maim as well as another, other things being equal, he would reject it and use the type that satisfies his intent to kill and grievously harm. The intent to kill as a means of terrorizing solves the problem deliberation poses of how to achieve victory. Turning to its direction of fit, if he were to drop the bombs and not kill or seriously harm the non-combatants, he would fail to do what he had intended. Again, this is true even if he were to cause the enemy to believe that he did terror bomb and thereby demoralizes them. For he sought to demoralize them by killing and gravely harming non-combatants. Again, if he were to lack the intent to terrorize by killing non-combatants (perhaps he erroneously believes the non-combatants to be soldiers and intends to kill them) his bombing must be redefined. For the intent to kill as a means of terrorizing denominates an act as terror bombing. Moreover, in such a case, his conduct would typically differ. For example, erroneously thinking he is bombing soldiers capable of defending themselves, he would bomb from a higher altitude. In light of these factors, terror bombing necessarily instantiates the intent to kill and grievously harm non-combatants as a means to victory.

The tactical bomber, like the terror bomber, ultimately intends victory. He differs from the terror bomber insofar as he foresees, but does not intend the foreseen non-combatant deaths and serious harms that follow with causal necessity from his destruction of the military installation. This is so, although the killing of the non-combatants may conduce to victory.[22] For the tactical bomber does not intend to achieve victory by means of non-combatant deaths. His foresight of civilian deaths and injuries does not guide his act; he does not confirm the presence of civilians to bomb them. As

[22] As noted in sec. 1.3, in light of this consideration, one does not present DER as holding that the harmful effect may not produce the good. For from the fact that the harm in part causes the good the agent intends (as in the case of tactical bombing's demoralizing of the enemy partially leading to victory) one may not conclude that the agent intends the harm. Of course, as Domingo de Sta Teresa insists (Mangan 1949, 57), the harmful effect cannot be the sole cause of the good. For a knowledgeable agent intending the good would thereby intend the harm (as the only means to the good).

opponents of DER might note, however, he may find the artillery installation in terms of its position relative to the civilians (for example, when smoke enshrouds the enemy's artillery while children on a nearby playground remain visible). This appears to indicate that his foresight of harm to the children directs his act. In fact, however, his act follows his intent to destroy the artillery installation. For it is the position of the children relative to the enemy artillery that interests him. Moreover, killing the children does not solve his deliberative problem of how to destroy the artillery. Again, in terms of direction of fit, if he were not to kill children, he would not thereby fail, although he incorrectly foresaw their deaths. The tactical bomber is not but could be ignorant that his bombs kill and gravely injure children. If he were, he would still properly be said to bomb tactically; moreover, he need change no feature of his act (the bombs he uses, the time when, or the altitude from which he bombs).

Thus, the i/f distinction applies to the classically contrasted cases as proponents argue. That is, in the cases of euthanasia/terminal sedation, craniotomy/hysterectomy, and terror bombing/tactical bombing, DER rightly classifies the first member of each pair as intentional harming and the second as foreseen and not intentional harming. This does not end the philosophical controversy, however. For what ethical relevance, if any, does this distinction have? In Chapter 4 I argue for the most controversial claim attending DER: that is, the ethical import of the distinction between intent of a means and foresight of a causally necessitated consequentially comparable concomitant.

4

The i/f distinction's ethical import

In Chapter 3 I considered how one both distinguishes intent from foresight and applies the distinction to the classic cases. While disputed, thinkers do not consider these the most controversial claims of DER. The fundamental disagreement concerns the ethical relevance of this distinction. Common morality and its advocates who employ DER hold that acts have numerous morally significant features; for example, intent, motive, and consequences. In contrast, consequentialism asserts that in evaluating an act consequences alone matter. Therefore, from a consequentialist standpoint, the i/f distinction lacks relevance in evaluating an action. For whether one foresees or intends a consequence need not affect the outcome. Thus, the i/f distinction represents one of the principal conflicted points regarding consequentialism's grounding claim. Accordingly, while some doubt the ethical import of the distinction, none doubt the importance of the debate concerning its significance.

4.1. COMMON MISUNDERSTANDINGS OF THE I/F DISTINCTION'S RELEVANCE

I now engage that debate by first considering certain (understandable) misunderstandings of the ethical import of the distinction. After considering these positions, I propose both act- and victim-focused accounts of its relevance.

4.1.1. Varying probabilities?

H. L. A. Hart understands proponents of DER as employing the i/f distinction to mark a difference in the probability of intended and foreseen consequences. Speaking of the craniotomy/hysterectomy cases, he says:

> if the craniotomy is contrasted with the removal of the womb containing the foetus as a case of 'direct' killing it must be on the basis that the death of the foetus is not merely contingently connected with craniotomy as it is with the removal of the womb containing it. But it is not clear that the supposition of the survival of the foetus makes better sense in the one case than in the other. (Hart 1967, 13)

Hart rightly rejects the position that the distinction has ethical relevance due to the disparate probabilities of death in the two cases. It is no more possible for a non-viable foetus to live when the uterus has been surgically removed from the mother than it is for a foetus to live when its head has been crushed. Of course, controversy attends the distinction precisely insofar as its proponents employ it to differentiate causally necessary consequentially comparable harms. Understandably, nevertheless incorrectly, Hart supposes that varying probabilities alone could serve as the basis for the distinction's ethical significance.

4.1.2. Full versus partial responsibility?

Some assert that the distinction lacks ethical relevance since it does not mark an ethically significant difference in an agent's responsibility for causing harm. Because this misunderstanding attends DER, I now consider it. As I argue, the distinction does not (nor does it attempt to) contrast varying degrees of responsibility that agents have for acts. Rather, as I indicate here, and argue at greater length in section 4.3, it concerns ethically relevant differences of which acts admit.

For example, concerning the terror-bomber/tactical bomber cases, someone might mistakenly think that proponents understand the distinction as marking varying degrees of responsibility (full versus partial) that agents have for causing harm intentionally or with foresight.[1] Yet,

---

[1] Some critics of DER make this error. One advocate of double effect (loosely and infelicitously) asks, '*why* should we consider ourselves far more responsible for what we do (or permit) intentionally than for consequences of action that we foresee and decide to accept but that do not form part of our aims (intermediate or final)? How can the connection of ends and means conduct responsibility so much more effectively than the connection of foresight and avoidability?' (Nagel 1980, 130, original emphasis) It becomes clear from the entire passage that Nagel does not finally hold what he here initially implies. That is, that the intended differs from the foreseen in terms of differing degrees of responsibility. Rather, as I note in sec. 4.3.1, he argues that intending evil ethically differs from foreseeing evil in terms of what evil means (see ibid. 132).

insofar as an agent's believing that a consequence follows from his act establishes his responsibility, the two cases do not differ in terms of responsibility. If the distinction attempts to contrast the two bombers in terms of their responsibility for dead non-combatants, it clearly fails. For each has full responsibility.

The assumption that the distinction contrasts varying degrees of responsibility is false. The i/f distinction concerns, not a difference in responsibility for acts, but different acts for which agents have responsibility. Recall that, *ex hypothesi*, terror- and tactical bombing, for example, cause the same amount of harm with the same probability. Moreover, (as noted in section 3.4.2) neither terror- nor tactical bombing instantiates an intent not to harm the non-combatants. Expanding on the points made in section 3.4.2, this is clearly true of terror bombing. For an act does not (at the same time and in the same respect) incorporate the intent both to harm and not to harm. Therefore, terror bombing does not instance the intent not to harm the non-combatants. Nor does tactical bombing. For an agent does not (rationally) intend not to cause what he knows he will in fact cause. Therefore, neither terror- nor tactical bombing instance the intent of not harming the non-combatants. Thus, terror- and tactical bombing share two ethically relevant characteristics insofar as both actions instantiate consequentially comparable voluntary harming and neither action instantiates the intention to benefit or not to harm. Yet, DER theorists understand the i/f distinction to mark an ethically important difference between these acts. What is this?

Insofar as terror bombing involves the intention to harm non-combatants, it is a malicious act. Of course, it is not an instance of harming just for the sake of harming; it is not sadistic. Similarly, tactical bombing does not incorporate harm to the non-combatants just for the sake of harming them. However, unlike terror bombing, it does not order their harm to the good of victory. As noted in section 1.3, this point holds even when harming the non-combatants helps to achieve victory. For the point is not whether harming the non-combatants contributes to victory; rather, the point is whether tactical bombing instances harming the non-combatants as a means to victory, as terror bombing does. In this respect, these two acts differ. Clearly, the agents who perform them have full responsibility. They have full responsibility, however, for different acts. The tactical bomber has complete responsibility for a non-malicious, non-beneficent act while the terror bomber has full responsibility for a malicious act. Since, prima facie, a non-malicious, non-beneficent act ethically differs from a malicious act, one reasonably thinks that the i/f distinction has ethical relevance insofar as it tracks this difference. Of course, this is not to argue that the distinction has ethical import. Rather, it establishes at the outset that one does not find that significance in varying degrees of responsibility.

4.2. THE FIRST-ORDER/SECOND-ORDER DISTINCTION

There remains one common construal of the i/f distinction's ethical relevance; namely, the position that the distinction lacks ethical relevance as applied to acts while having import as applied to agents. I now consider this claim. Giving the i/f distinction moral weight in one's evaluation of acts amounts to holding that differences in volition (specifically, the differences between willing harm as a means and willing harm as a concomitant of what one wills as an end or means) ground differences in the evaluation of acts with otherwise similar consequences. Some recent thinkers, however, hold that volitional states lack relevance in act-evaluation while holding that if volitional states have relevance, it is to be found in the evaluation of agents. (Proponents of this claim often speak of act-evaluation as the first-order and agent-evaluation as the second-order of morality.)[2] These thinkers divorce the ethical assessment of actions from that of agents. Accordingly, they understand there to be a significant gap between the criteria for evaluating an action and those for evaluating an agent. In accordance with this position, some hold that while, for example, terror bombing is no worse than tactical bombing, the terror bomber might be worse than the tactical bomber. They hold this, not because he does something worse, but because, at least proximately, something worse motivates him (the deaths and terror of non-combatants) than what motivates the tactical bomber (the destruction of a military installation). More generally, this position comes to holding that one judges acts without reference to the agent's epistemic and volitional states while one evaluates agents partially in

[2] See e.g. Donagan (1977), 52–74 and 112–31; Bennett (1995), 46–61 and 194–6; and Frankena (1980), 48–54. Mill addresses the point in the second edition of *Utilitarianism*, ch. II, fn. 2.

terms of their epistemic and volitional states. Those who think that DER mistakenly contrasts acts such as terror- and tactical bombing often hold that it conflates act-evaluation with agent-assessment. Thus, the position that the first-order/second-order distinction marks a gap between act-and agent-evaluations bears on the debate concerning the ethical relevance of the i/f distinction and the tenability of DER. I now turn to the destructive task of articulating and criticizing the first-order/second-order distinction understood dichotomously. Upon removing this obstacle, I attend to the constructive goal of arguing for the ethical relevance of the distinction. The destructive task begins with a brief consideration of what constitutes a human action.

4.2.1. The first-order/second-order distinction and morality's breadth: the voluntary

Fundamentally, ethics concerns the goodness and badness of what humans knowingly and willingly (or, voluntarily) cause or allow. Ethics concentrates exclusively on the voluntary. A knowing-willing-causing excludes what one causes in inculpable ignorance and what one causes by force.[3] An agent is culpably ignorant when he does not know what he can know but knowingly and willingly chooses not to know. For example, when Joe finds a wallet full of money and

---

[3] The same can be said for knowing-willing-allowings, which I put aside for the moment. I rely on Aristotle's classic account of the voluntary found in the *Nicomachean Ethics*, book III, chs. 1–5.

chooses not to investigate whose wallet he has found, he is voluntarily and thereby culpably ignorant of whose money he takes. Moreover, an agent is culpable for her ignorance when she does not know something she can know and has the responsibility to know. For example, if Mary is a physician, she has the responsibility to know if her patient is allergic to penicillin before she administers it. The obligation to know is voluntary insofar as it attends her voluntarily being a doctor.

Knowledge and volition bound ethics. They define morality's breadth, extension, or range. In order for something to be considered within ethics, it must fall within the boundaries constituted by knowledge and volition. Shortly (in section 4.3.1), I argue that morality also has a depth that differences in volition partially establish and demarcate. In terms of these volitional differences, one contrasts consequentially comparable acts as better or worse and justifiable or not justifiable. Before making this argument, I present the first-order/second-order distinction as some understand it to mark a gap between act- and agent-evaluation. Relying on the above general account of human action, I criticize the dichotomous understanding of this distinction.[4] Thus, my criticism of the first-order/second-order distinction

---

[4] I do not, of course, object to distinguishing evaluations of acts from those of agents. Rather, I reject the assertion that one can evaluate an act without reference to an agent's epistemic and volitional dispositions. I consider this a dichotomous understanding of the distinction. Moreover, I would not describe this as a distinction between different orders of morality (which leads, naturally, to the position that the first-order comes first). Agents and acts arise simultaneously; evaluations of the one typically bear upon the other.

understood dichotomously follows from what I take to be a shared account of what a human action is most generally, a knowing-willing. This general account of human action undermines a dichotomous understanding of the first-order/second-order distinction. Moreover, this account of action grounds the ethical import of the i/f distinction.

4.2.2.   The first-order/second-order distinction: Donagan

Alan Donagan says that first-order moral questions concern actions as permissible or impermissible and second-order moral questions concern 'the culpability or inculpability of agents' (Donagan 1977, 55). He describes this distinction, saying:

The distinction between first-order and second-order moral questions is related to a distinction...between actions considered materially and actions considered formally. Considered materially, an action is a deed, and *no reference is made to the doer's state of mind* in doing it. Thus, an action is material stealing, or materially considered is stealing, if it is the forcible or surreptitious taking of what belongs to somebody else. Considered formally, an action is what its doer wills to do in doing it. Hence an action which materially is stealing may not be so formally, because the stealer may honestly believe that what he is taking is his own property. (ibid., emphasis added)

According to Donagan, first-order morality considers effects attributable to an agent without reference to the agent's epistemic and volitional states. Second-order morality considers the agent's mental states regarding actions evaluated in first-order morality. He understands first-order morality to concern actions insofar as they are the effects of human beings as causes, not insofar as they are agents or knowing-willing-causes.

Donagan holds that an action considered materially has no reference to the agent's beliefs or wants. Yet, to consider an action materially is to consider an action. When one considers an action, one considers a knowing-willing-causing. Of course, one can ask whether what an agent does is permissible or impermissible without asking, for example, why he does it. Nonetheless, to ask whether what an agent does is permissible or impermissible requires a reference to his epistemic and volitional states, which states either establish his responsibility for a specific act or indicate that no act occurred. If no act occurred, then nothing permissible or impermissible occurred.

If one could evaluate an act without reference to an agent's mental states, there would seem to be a substantial gap between the criteria in terms of which one evaluates an act and the conditions establishing an agent's responsibility. In fact, this is Donagan's position, as he states, 'our analysis ... has shown that a prescription of practical reason that somebody not do an action of a certain kind does not entail a prescription that he be blamed if he does it. A deed may be impermissible, and yet its doer be inculpable; and a doer may be culpable even though his deed is permissible' (ibid. 112). Donagan presents two kinds of cases: first, an agent inculpably doing an impermissible deed; second, an agent culpably doing a permissible deed.

Concerning the first case, one can cause something bad that would be impermissible to cause if one were to cause it voluntarily. For example, if in inculpable ignorance I ruin your freshly poured concrete driveway, you can say, 'if he had ruined the driveway voluntarily, it would have been wrong'. However, to say this is not to evaluate ruining the driveway without reference to an agent's epistemic and volitional states. For 'it' refers to voluntarily or knowingly-willingly ruining the driveway.

As Anscombe says:

Naturally, a rule as you consider it in deciding to obey or disobey it does not run: do not *voluntarily* do such-and-such, for you cannot consider whether to do such-and-such voluntarily or not.... The voluntariness is presupposed in [the agent's] *considering whether* to do [the act]. Thus it does not come into his considerations of what to do... (Anscombe 1981, 8, original emphases)

The voluntary serves as morality's threshold. Thus, once inside morality, we attend, implicitly or explicitly, to the voluntary. My inculpably ruining your driveway is like a tree's doing so; it is not voluntary. My so ruining it, however, is more easily conflated with my voluntarily and wrongly doing so because while both a tree and I can ruin your driveway, only I can voluntarily (or involuntarily) ruin it. To see the point, consider the incongruity of saying 'what the tree did was impermissible'. What the tree did is more clearly not an act than what I involuntarily caused. Nonetheless, the latter is no more an act than the former. Thus, we err when we speak of my involuntarily ruining your driveway as an impermissible act. Indeed, although easily confused with one, it is no act at all, and, therefore, neither permissible nor impermissible.[5]

The second case Donagan mentions concerns an agent being culpable although his act is permissible. For example, the act of giving food to a hungry person described to that partial extent is permissible, indeed, commendable. Speaking of this act as permissible, however, anticipates the usual good reasons on account of which one gives food to the hungry (for example, to relieve hunger). I am blamed when the reason I give food was to get the hungry man to commit a crime. I am not blamed, however, for the permissible act. Indeed, I did not even do the permissible act. For the permissible act is the fully described one of feeding the hungry for some unobjectionable reason. Conceptually, when one performs a permissible act one cannot be to blame for it. Thus, in the two types of acts that Donagan describes, it is conceptually the case that one cannot blame an agent for an act that is permissible nor can one hold that an agent's act was impermissible while asserting that he was not to blame. In short, the criteria of act-evaluation cannot be entirely divorced from the criteria in terms of which agents are responsible for acts.

Once one acknowledges that an act, because it is a knowing-willing-causing, cannot be evaluated without reference to an agent's epistemic and volitional states and that these states establish an agent's responsibility for the

---

[5] Of course, my involuntarily ruining your driveway may accompany my act of delivering the pizza you ordered (while forgetting to tell me about the new concrete), or of looking for my dog.

act, then the putative gap between act- and agent-evaluation closes. When understood as marking a dichotomy, the first-order/second-order distinction faces a conceptually insuperable difficulty; namely, to speak of an act necessarily constituted by epistemic and volitional states without reference to those very states.

4.2.3.   The first-order/second-order distinction: Bennett

Jonathan Bennett explicitly follows Donagan in holding that the first-order/second-order distinction marks a dichotomy. According to Bennett, first-order morality in no way considers the mental states of agents. He says, 'the meanings of the transitive verbs in our standard repertoire [of first-order morality] are silent about what Agent knew or wanted, and therefore about what he intended; so the source of an emphasis on intention must be sought elsewhere' (Bennett 1995, 45). According to him, since first-order morality makes no reference to an agent's mental states, intention cannot bear on act-evaluation. He holds that if intention has significance it would be in agent-assessment.[6]

What are the transitive verbs of which he speaks? He gives as examples, ' "hurt", "help", "betray", "reward", and "harm" ' (ibid.). Thus, according to Bennett, to say "I hurt him" is to remain silent about what I knew or wanted. A plea

---

[6] Ultimately, Bennett thinks that the distinction lacks ethical relevance in agent-assessment when applied to consequentially comparable cases (Bennett 1995, 221–4).

for excuses is in order. Bennett's position comes to holding that the only excuse to the accusation of hurting, for example, would be to say 'it did not really hurt'—which surely adds insult to injury. That is, the only excuse would be to comment on resulting states of affairs, never to refer to mental states. Yet, to an accusation of hurting, the accused might respond, 'I did not know that it hurt', or 'I knew, but I did not want to hurt you'. The accuser implies that the verb applies. The excuser can assert that it does not apply because he did not know, and, therefore, as described, that action did not occur. Or, he can assert that he knew but did not want to hurt, and, therefore, 'hurting' does not entirely describe his act insofar as it implies that he sought to cause harm.

The accused is not mistaken to focus on his epistemic and volitional states in responding to the accusations. For the vocabulary of common morality speaks of epistemic and volitional states. It is, however, at times vague and ambiguous insofar as I can cause you harm without knowing or wanting. Yet, to cause you harm without knowing that what I cause is harmful is not an act of hurting. In fact, to cause some upshot without thinking will at times not be to act at all, for example, if while sleepwalking I bump you. Moreover, to cause you pain without willing to is not (without qualification) to hurt you. For example, if I am a physician and the shot I give you hurts, I may note that although I knew that it would hurt, that was not my goal. I concede that I caused you pain and to that extent hurt you, but I deny that I hurt you insofar as hurting implies wanting to hurt.

If you accept excuses that refer to my beliefs and desires then you understand the verb at issue to refer to my epistemic and volitional states, amongst other things. Since ordinary users of ordinary language do accept such excuses we have reason to hold that the vocabulary of morality is not silent about what Agent knew or wanted, and, therefore, is not silent about what he intended. In evaluating acts one appropriately (indeed, as I argue shortly, necessarily) attends to knowledge and will, and, thereby, to intent.

4.2.4.   Two sources of the error

What leads some to think that one could evaluate an act without referring to the agent's epistemic and volitional states? This error appears to have two sources. The first is ontological, arising from the fact that states of affairs partially constitute acts. The second comes from tacitness, or how we speak about acts. Consider them in order.

States of affairs are objectively good or bad. For example, a hungry person's having food is good. Of course, to hold this we need not refer to any agent's beliefs or desires about the hungry having food. Indeed, the goodness of states of affairs such as the goodness of the hungry having food causes us to have beliefs and desires about the goodness and desirability of the hungry having food. If I walk down the street with a bag full of bagels and, without my knowing or willing it, one falls out and rolls down the sidewalk to a homeless hungry man, this is good. I, however, am not involved as an agent. The bagel's rolling down the sidewalk is not my act. Indeed, it is not an act. Nonetheless, it might be good insofar as it brings about the hungry man's being fed. To say that it is good, regardless of my beliefs and desires, that the bagel rolls down the sidewalk to the hungry man, is not to say that there is some act that can be evaluated as good without reference to my beliefs and desires. The error—call it the ontological fallacy—occurs in thinking that one can speak of actions as being ethically good or bad without reference to an agent's beliefs and desires. One might erroneously think this insofar as, without reference to an agent's beliefs and desires, one can speak of good and bad states of affairs that would partially constitute actions as ethically good or bad if they were caused knowingly and willingly. However, when they are not caused voluntarily, one cannot speak of these good and bad states of affairs as being ethically good or bad, permissible or impermissible acts.

Another cause of the dichotomous understanding of the first-order/second-order distinction surrounds what Bennett speaks of as the silence of first-order morality concerning agents's beliefs, desires, and intents. As Anscombe notes, we do not normally say 'do not *voluntarily* φ'. Similarly, we do not usually say 'do not *knowingly* or *willingly* or *intentionally* φ'. This has led some to hold that first-order morality excludes consideration of agent's knowledge, will, and intent. Indeed, the exact opposite is the case. Take, for example, the verb 'reward' that Bennett considers. Only in a peculiar case does one draw attention to the voluntary nature of one's rewarding another. For example, when upon your returning my wallet, I say 'I reward you voluntarily', I thereby highlight the willingness with which I do so. I do so with relish.[7] First-order morality incorporates reference to agents's beliefs, desires, and intentions. Indeed, it does so so customarily that the incorporation remains tacit. This silence, however, is not to be taken for an absence; rather, it indicates a taken-for-granted presence.

4.3. THE DISTINCTION'S ETHICAL RELEVANCE

I now begin my positive account of the i/f distinction's ethical relevance. As will become evident, the i/f distinction has two facets to its ethical import: that of intent itself and that of intent vis-à-vis the person victimized by the act. The first concerns the act itself; rests on broadly Aristotelian-Thomistic grounds; and mirrors the basic truth that what makes an act to be an act in part makes it to be a good or bad act. That is, because volition partially constitutes an act as an act, differences in volition (specifically, the difference between intent and foresight) make otherwise comparable acts better or worse. In terms of the first facet, one claims that intent of some good or bad effect makes for a better or worse act than would foresight of the same. The second facet regards the victim of the act; has Kantian grounds; and reflects the moral status of persons as never properly treated

---

[7] Italian captures the sense in its use of *volentiere* to refer to instances in which the speaker performs an action he particularly desires to do.

as mere means.[8] I now turn to the first aspect of the distinction's significance.

4.3.1. Morality's depth and volitional states

As noted in section 4.2.1, an agent's knowing-willing demarcates morality's breadth or subject matter, the voluntary. The sine qua non for moral relevance is an agent's having certain epistemic and volitional states. Yet, while moral import begins with these states, it does not end there. For ethics also has a depth in terms of which we speak of acts as better or worse, or in terms of which we evaluate acts.

To begin with a point widely agreed upon—and championed by consequentialists—other things being equal, that an act brings about more good or evil than another makes it to be a better or worse act. Upon establishing the voluntary character of some outcome, consequentialists focus entirely upon the magnitude of the goodness or badness of the outcome to determine the goodness or badness of the act. They correctly advance the quantity of the effect's goodness or badness as being morally relevant. (For, again as noted in section 4.2.1, ethics is about voluntary *outcomes* (caused or allowed). Certainly, one partially evaluates a good or bad

---

[8] I call the first aspect of the distinction Aristotelian insofar as it presupposes Aristotle's account of the voluntary found in *Nicomachean Ethics*, book III, chs. 1–5. It is Thomistic insofar as it develops Aquinas's claim that intent is essential in act-analysis (*Summa theologiae* I-II, q.12). The victim-focused aspect of the distinction is Kantian in terms of the end-not-means formulation of the Categorical Imperative.

outcome quantitatively.) Consequentialists err in their act-evaluations, however, in entirely ignoring the different volitional states bearing upon the outcome. Acknowledging that volitional relations have a crucial role to play in establishing moral significance, once such relations have been confirmed they rush on ahead, as it were, impatient to evaluate the magnitude of the effect and abandoning as insignificant the different ways in which an effect can be willed. In what follows, I argue that insofar as epistemic and volitional states bearing upon an effect make that effect to have any moral import whatsoever, differences in volitional states bearing upon that effect make for differences in the moral significance of that effect. To the extent to which the i/f distinction marks these differences, it has moral weight.

Recall that the controversy concerning the ethical relevance of the distinction centres particularly on the contrast between what one wills as a means and what one foresees as a concomitant. To establish this difference, I focus on three distinct volitional states: willing something as an end, for its own sake; willing something as a means, as ordered to the realization of one's end; and willing something as a concomitant either of one's end or of one's means, solely as associated with one's end or means.

I here and throughout the following employ 'will' to denote the agent's having a volitional disposition towards an outcome of his act. The volitional dispositions bearing on ends, means, and concomitants of ends and means differ. As Aquinas notes, and as discussed in section 3.4.2, we speak most precisely of willing an end, choosing means, and intending ends through means. No word exactly captures the volitional relationship to foreseen concomitants. As argued in section 3.1.3, some terms certainly will not do; 'accept', 'permit', and 'allow' suffer the defect of connoting another's agency in contrast to one's own. 'Assent' comes to mind as a more technical term that might serve as it nicely contrasts with choosing and intending. One notes, however, that it, too, has the flaw of indicating acquiescence to another's agency. For reasons noted in section 3.1, I am loath to employ terms that might diminish acknowledgment of the agent's full responsibility for the concomitant. Accordingly, I settle for the noted imprecision of 'will' while offering the following arguments to indicate how the agent's volitional disposition towards a concomitant ethically differs from that towards an end or means.

As noted in section 3.4, the three volitional states bearing on ends, means, and concomitants relate to one another causally. One wills an end for its own sake. This willing of an end causes one to deliberate about means, and, upon discovering them, to choose and intend them in a plan of action. One wills means as chosen and intended for the sake of the end. For example, when I want to catch fish, I must employ some means of doing so: a net; or a rod, reel, and lure. My wanting to catch fish leads me to choose and intend means: this lure and this pole. What one wills as an end may also cause one to will something else as a concomitant. For example, my wanting to catch fish may also cause me to bring a good fishing-spot to the notice of other fishermen. Thus, my end determines what I will, choose, and intend as a means and sometimes itself determines what I will as a concomitant. What one wills, chooses, and intends as a means does not have a causal influence on what one wills as an end. It does, however, sometimes itself determine what else one wills as a concomitant. For example, in choosing to catch fish by means of a lure, I know that as a side effect I will snag seaweed. I will to snag seaweed as a concomitant. Thus, both what one wills as a means and what one wills as an end determine what one wills as a concomitant. What one wills as a concomitant, however, does not determine what one wills as an end or as a means. I will the concomitant neither for its own sake nor for the sake of something else (for it does not advance or serve my purpose). I neither choose nor intend it in my plan of action. Rather, I will it in an entirely derivative, superficial, and secondary fashion as inevitably causally associated with what I will primarily.

Insofar as what an agent knowingly and willingly causes constitutes an action and insofar as willing admits of these three distinct relations, the goodness and badness of actions that cause consequentially similar states of affairs vary partly in accordance with the different volitional states that constitute different actions. That is, other things being equal, an action that brings about a bad state of affairs as an end is worse (more profoundly wrong) than one that brings a consequentially similar bad state of affairs about as a means. Moreover, an act that brings a bad state of affairs about as a concomitant is not as bad (it may even be good) as the acts that bring similar consequences about as an end or as a means. In short, goodness and badness of acts vary in part with the different volitional states with which agents will good and bad states of affairs. For the action is in part that volitional state regarding that good or bad state of affairs.

For example, the tactical bomber would rather cause the deaths of the non-combatants than forgo destroying the military installation. He wills their deaths as a concomitant. This willing of their deaths derives entirely from his wanting to destroy the military installation as an end and no further willing derives from his willing their deaths. For example, he does not choose some type of bomb in order to kill the non-combatants.[9] The willing of non-combatant deaths attending tactical bombing is superficial and entirely derivative in contrast to the willing of non-combatant deaths that constitutes terror bombing. Terror bombing consists of willing terror and non-combatant deaths as means to the end of victory (intending them as means). The prospect of non-combatant deaths and terror causes and defines terror bombing. Terror bombing instantiates a qualitatively different wanting of terror and non-combatant deaths than does tactical bombing. Accordingly, other things being equal, terror bombing is worse than tactical bombing.

If there were some third type of bombing the goal of which were solely to kill and terrorize non-combatants (call it sadistic bombing) this would surely be worse than both terror and tactical bombing. But why? Other things being equal, it cannot be worse in terms of its consequences. It is worse, and the worst kind of bombing (most profoundly wrong), because it instantiates the paradigmatic

---

[9] Although, as noted in sec. 3.4.2, his willing of their deaths as a causally necessitated concomitant prevents him from intending not to kill them.

form of wanting, but does so with respect towards something bad. For in sadistic bombing the terror and deaths of the non-combatants are ends in themselves, sought for their own sake. Other things being equal, sadistic bombing is worse than terror bombing and terror bombing is worse than tactical bombing. These comparative relationships hold insofar as these acts instantiate distinct volitional attitudes towards otherwise similar outcomes. These differences partially measure morality's depth (as would in their own way, for example, differences in consequences).[10] In short, different volitional attitudes towards consequentially similar resulting states of affairs make for differences in act-evaluation.

As we have seen, however, this position is controverted. For example, Bennett says:

if a first-order morality's basic concern is to oppose behaviour that has relational property RP, that does not give it a derivative concern with beliefs about or attitudes towards RP. For example, a morality's having a basic concern with the causing of pain does not give it a derivative concern with beliefs about the causing of pain. Such beliefs are relevant to judgements in the associated second-order morality, but not to first-order judgements of wrongness. (Bennett 1995, 49)

According to Bennett, if some ethic were to oppose the causing of pain, it should not have any concern about an agent's volitional states concerning the causing of pain in the

---

[10] For example, if there were no difference in volitional relations to the outcomes, but the outcomes quantitatively differed such that one instance of sadistic bombing killed more than another, it would be worse.

assessment of an action because volitional states are not relevant in act-evaluation. Yet, in an ethic fundamentally opposed to causing pain, causing pain just for the sake of causing pain is the worst act because to want something for its own sake is to want it paradigmatically. Therefore, an act instantiating the willing as an end of what ought to be avoided is most profoundly wrong. This truth cannot be captured, however, if first-order morality consists only of what an agent knowingly and willingly brings about without reference to distinct volitional states. For to bring something about as an end, or as a means, or as a side-effect is to bring it about voluntarily or knowingly and willingly. If one does not differentiate these distinct volitional states that partially constitute actions, then one's act-evaluations remain superficial insofar as they do not plumb morality's other dimension that differences in volition partially measure—depth (as they would remain incomplete if they failed to take into account, for example, the magnitude of the good or bad effected by the act).

To see the point in another way, consider biology's first distinction, that between the living and the non-living. Biologists note certain characteristics in terms of which one demarcates biology's subject matter from what falls outside of its purview. So, for example, the living contrasts from the non-living insofar as it moves itself, moderates itself (homeostasis), reproduces, and so on. The characteristics in terms of which biologists distinguish the living from the non-living determine biology's breadth. Like ethics, biology also has a depth in terms of which one differentiates living things from one another. Biologists first measure this

depth in terms of the variations of which those characteristics that differentiate the living from the inert admit. So,
for example, to the extent to which some living things fly,
others swim, and still others move on land, biologists take
into account these differences of self-motion as they make
distinctions within biology's borders (again, those very borders established by the original criteria differentiating the
living from the non-living). The original criteria ramify and
thereby mark differences amongst the living. So the cold-
blooded contrast with the warm-blooded in terms of
homeostasis and those that reproduce sexually from those
that do so asexually, and so on. It would be an odd taxonomy that did not first take into account the differences of
which the most important and fundamental distinctions
(those used to distinguish the living from the non-living)
admit in classifying and specifying living organisms. So also,
it would be a fundamentally inconsistent ethic that did not
take into account the differences of which its very first
distinction (knowing-willing, or the voluntary) admits in
evaluating acts.

One who holds that differences in willing do not make for
differences in act-assessments must explain why knowing
and willing define an act in contrast to a happening (and
thereby demarcate ethics's subject matter), yet the variations
of which willing admits lack relevance in act-assessment. For
ethics has nothing to say (about me or what I cause) when
I harm or help you in inculpable ignorance or by force and
without willing to (say someone pushes me into you), while
it speaks volumes when I knowingly and willingly harm or
help you. It puzzles and goes against sound taxonomy to

hold that harm or benefit coming about in accordance with volition has fundamental importance in ethics (by establishing that an act occurred) while holding that further differences of which willing admits make no difference at all in act-evaluation. Such a position is out of step with ethics's originating concern with human knowing-willings, or, in other words, the voluntary. Because the goodness and badness of states of affairs have moral import and enter into act-evaluation only insofar as agents knowingly and willingly cause or allow those states of affairs, the differences of which willing admits (as an end, as a means, or as a concomitant) constitute differences in act-evaluation. Thus, actions are right or wrong and better or worse partially in terms of these different volitional states.

An opponent of DER might concede that the relationships I argue for hold—that, for example, sadistic bombing is worse than terror bombing which, in turn, is worse than tactical bombing. Yet, he might ask, why draw the line, as DER does, between the impermissible and the permissible so as to separate terror from tactical bombing? Why not draw the line (as opponents of DER might suggest) between sadistic and terror bombing? Could one not agree that sadistic bombing is impermissible while holding that one may terror bomb, conceding that it is worse (and thereby requires a greater justification) than consequentially comparable tactical bombing, but not impermissible?

Nagel offers the basis for a reply. He says:

to aim at evil, *even as a means,* is to have one's action *guided* by evil. One must be prepared to adjust it to insure the production of evil: a falling off in the level of the desired evil must be grounds for altering what one does so that the evil is restored and maintained. But the *essence* of evil is that it should *repel* us. If something is evil, our actions should be guided, if they are guided by it at all, toward its elimination rather than towards its maintenance. That is what evil *means*. So when we aim at evil we are swimming head-on against the normative current. Our action is guided by the goal at every point in the direction diametrically opposite to that in which the value of that goal points. To put it another way, if we aim at evil we make what we do in the first instance a positive rather than a negative function of evil. At every point, the intentional function is simply the normative function reversed... (Nagel 1980, 132–3, original emphases)

Nagel eloquently, albeit partially, echoes Aquinas's articulation of the first ethical principle, 'do good and avoid evil' (I-II q.94 a.2). As noted in section 4.2.1, this principle proposes (as do all ethical norms) that we voluntarily do good and avoid evil. Yet, a hard fact of life confronts one who sets out both to do good and avoid evil: their occasional incompatibility. One cannot heal the patient without pain or discipline the child without tears. In short, one cannot without qualification do good and avoid evil. How ought we to act when the doing of good involves a failure to avoid evil and the avoidance of evil involves a failure to do good?

We ought deliberately and intentionally do good and avoid evil. We ought to intend the good, that is, deliberately pursue it. When it comes to understanding our proper relation to evil, we ought, deliberately and intentionally, to avoid it. We ought to intend to avoid evil. Yet, what of those instances when intending to avoid evil would prevent us from intending to do good? For example, the oncologist cannot intend to avoid nauseating, debilitating, and generally sickening his patient while also intending to heal his patient by means of chemotherapy. Is he, therefore, not to administer this therapy? Of course not. For one can intend to avoid evil and one can avoid intending evil. At first, we ought to intend to avoid evil: deliberate about how not to cause or allow it. The oncologist should seek that therapy that avoids sickening his patient while also curing. If he were to use a therapy that sickened his patient when another (comparable but for its not sickening his patient) were available, he would have acted wrongly in not avoiding evil (by deliberating about how and intending to avoid evil). However, if no other comparable therapy were available to cure but that which also sickened, then he need not forgo using that therapy in order to avoid evil. In such a case, his proper relation to evil is *not* to intend to avoid it; rather, he must not intend to sicken his patient. For the greater good of curing his patient justifies his not intending to avoid the causally necessitated concomitant evil; while evil's repulsive nature requires that he not intend it.

Therefore, when we cannot intend to avoid evil without sacrificing a comparable or greater good, we may intend and seek the good as long as we do not intend evil. If we intend evil, we set out for it as an intermediate, or worse, ultimate goal. All agree that Satan's 'evil, be thou my good' perverts the basic normative relationship that one ought to have towards evil. For evil's essence, as Nagel argues, ought to repel us, while Milton's Lucifer proposes it as an ultimate goal. Similarly—although not as perversely as Satan—when one intends evil as a means, one relates to evil as good. In relating to it as a good one inverts the proper volitional relation. What should repel, instead attracts us; this is wrong. If one does not intend to avoid evil when doing so requires one to forgo intending good, however, one does not thereby find evil good. Therefore, not to intend to avoid evil is not necessarily wrong. Accordingly, between failing to intend to avoid evil and intending evil one reasonably draws the line between permissible and impermissible volitional relations to evil while doing good.

Since one ought always to intend good and never to intend evil, and the world sometimes presents one with situations in which one cannot intend good and intend to avoid evil, one may intend good and not intend to avoid evil as long as one does not invert the basic normative relation to evil by intending it (and one satisfies the criteria noted in section 1.3). Given the nature of evil as what ought to repel, the i/f distinction rightly draws the line between impermissible and permissible acts resulting in good and evil. Moreover, this reasonably balances the doing of good and the avoidance of evil. For the good one ought to do limits one's intending to avoid evil; in turn, not intending evil constrains the good one ought to do. When good and evil inextricably bind, neither doing good nor avoiding evil alone suffices for an ethical act; one's act must incorporate both. Of course, the i/f distinction also applies to good consequences of one's act. Thus, when I refrain from eating the bread offered to me in a restaurant, foreseeing but not intending that it will go to a hungry homeless person, my restraint ethically differs from my not eating it with the intent that it feed the hungry

person. Other things being equal, intending good consequences is better than foreseeing while not intending them.
These relations further indicate the reasonableness of the i/f
distinction.[11]

Thus far, I have spoken of evil and of the different forms of
volition, focusing on the agent's volitional states and the evil
or harm constitutive of the acts considered in double effect.
To do so leaves one with the impression that there are only
volitional states towards harmful outcomes at issue in the
debate concerning DER. To hold this would be a serious
error. For in DER one speaks of evil more precisely as persons
victimized. This is the other facet of the i/f distinction's
ethical relevance whereby it illuminates the status of persons
and the wrongness of intentionally harming them.

4.3.2.   The Kantian insight

The Kantian insight that it is wrong to treat another human
being, an end-in-itself, merely as a means to furthering
some other end (the end-not-means principle) captures the
victim-focused aspect of the i/f distinction's ethical import.[12]
For example, according to DER, tactical bombing is

---

[11] See Nagel (1980), 132–3 for a different interpretation of the i/f
distinction and good consequences.

[12] Kant serves as the secular source of the end-not-means principle, which
enjoys a venerable history. A complete account of the principle's antecedents
would prominently feature Augustine's discussion of the difference between
use and enjoyment found in *De doctrina christiana*, I. For contemporary
reliance upon the principle, see Quinn (1989) and Kamm (1992).

permissible while terror bombing is not because tactical bombing does not treat non-combatants as mere means to the realization of an end while terror bombing does. Thus, terror bombing violates the end-not-means principle while tactical bombing does not.

Bennett, for one, finds this position implausible:

I can find no reading of the 'end, not means' principle which makes it both plausible and relevant to our present question [the ethical import of the intended/foreseen distinction]. If there is one, it must not only clear the tactical bomber of using the civilians as a means, but must imply that he is treating them as ends. Tell that to the civilians! (Bennett 1995, 218)

Bennett thinks that to contrast terror and tactical bombing in terms of the end-not-means principle it does not suffice that tactical bombing not use the non-combatants as means. Additionally, tactical bombing should treat them as ends by benefiting them. If Bennett were correct, the i/f distinction would not have ethical relevance in terms of the end-not-means principle. For, while tactical bombing does not use the civilians as a means, it not only fails to benefit them, it harms them. In effect, Bennett reads the end-not-means principle conjunctively as requiring that one *both* not treat others as just a means *and* that one treat them as ends by benefiting them.

I propose that the end-not-means principle be read disjunctively as laying it down that one is *either* (ideally) to benefit others (while, of course, not treating them as mere means) *or* (as a default from the ideal and as a bare minimum for ethically permissible conduct) one must not treat others as mere means.[13] That an act lives up to the ideal recommends it; that it meets the default does not rule it out. An act that does not benefit or that has the serious defect of concomitantly harming while not using others may, nevertheless, have countervailing reasons that conclusively argue for its performance. An act that treats others merely as means is wrong, although it have weighty reasons on its behalf. Thus, in response to Bennett, I hold that 'to treat another as an end' is ambiguous between treating others as ends by advancing their good and treating others as ends by not treating them merely as means. The disjunctive reading of the end-not-means principle clarifies this ambiguity. Moreover, as will become evident, the disjunctive reading captures nuances concerning the better and worse amongst acts judged to be right or wrong.

To illustrate the disjunctive reading of the end-not-means principle, consider the following types of bombing in an otherwise just war that cause consequentially comparable harm to non-combatants: relief bombing, risky tactical bombing, safe tactical bombing, eliminative bombing, terror bombing, and sadistic bombing.

One undertakes relief bombing to benefit non-combatants. A paradigm case of relief bombing is bombing that ends the

---

[13] By here saying 'while not treating them as mere means', I make what I hope is understood explicit for the sake of clarity and to allay the worries of those thinkers who propose that one could benefit another while treating him merely as a means. Here and throughout this section, (as noted in sec. 4.2 *et passim*) one benefits another not simply when one's act has the effect of benefiting him. Rather, one benefits another when the point of one's act is to do so. Thus, to benefit another excludes doing so while treating him merely as a means.

siege of a city occupied by civilians. The point of such bombing is to benefit them. Nonetheless, such bombing may harm some of the very people on whose behalf one undertakes it. For example, it may not be possible not to harm some of the non-combatants as one relieves the siege, for the forces laying siege to the city may be so close to the civilians that bombs dropped on the forces inevitably harm some non-combatants. Call relief bombing that harms some of the people on whose behalf it is undertaken harmful relief bombing.

As noted, one bombs tactically to destroy a military target. Tactical bombing may sometimes concomitantly harm non-combatants. Because a tactical bomber might be able to minimize such harm by placing himself at risk, two instances need to be distinguished. First, there is risky-non-combatant-harm-minimization-tactical-bombing, henceforth, risky tactical bombing. In risky tactical bombing, the tactical bomber places himself at risk in order to minimize harm to non-combatants. For example, the bomber may be able to minimize the harm by bombing from a low altitude that enables greater precision while posing risks to him.[14] In contrast to risky tactical bombing there is safe tactical

[14] As noted in sec. 1.3, Walzer argues that in cases to which double effect applies, when one can, one must bear risks in order to minimize the harm one foreseeably causes to others (Walzer 1977, 151–9). Read disjunctively, the end-not-means principle recommends risky tactical bombing. For, as risky, it satisfies the ideal in treating the non-combatants as ends, being undertaken partially on their behalf. However, the principle does not require such an act (as Walzer would). For one would not be treating the non-combatants as mere means if one were not to put oneself at risk. Of course, to act permissibly one must exercise due care to avoid harm. In some cases due care may dictate taking risks, in others not.

bombing. In safe tactical bombing, although he can, the tactical bomber does not take risks in order to minimize harm to civilians.

Eliminative bombing destroys non-combatants whose physical presence impedes the destruction of another legitimate military target.[15] In such cases, persons obstruct the achievement of one's goal; one begins to pursue that goal by destroying them.

Terror bombing harms, kills, and thereby terrorizes non-combatants as a means of lowering morale and achieving victory. In terror bombing, the killing, maiming, and subsequent terrifying of civilians are means of achieving victory. Of course, as considered in the debate concerning the ethical relevance of the i/f distinction, terror bombing excludes gratuitous harming of non-combatants. The terror bomber harms only to the extent necessary to achieve his goal.

Finally, there is sadistic bombing that kills and harms non-combatants for its own sake. Sadistic bombing may further some military goal, but it is not undertaken for the sake of such a goal.

A disjunctive reading of the end-not-means principle indicates that harmful relief bombing, risky tactical bombing, and safe tactical bombing are justifiable (given certain caveats, for example, a comparison of overall benefit to

[15] Although he does not use the examples of terror- and eliminative bombing, Quinn notes that DER and basic moral intuitions oppose what he calls opportunistic agency (in this instance, terror bombing) more than eliminative agency (Quinn 1989, 350). As will become evident, the disjunctive reading of the end-not-means principle indicates the basis for holding opportunistic agency to be the worse of these two objectionable ways of relating to persons.

overall harm) to the extent to which they meet the ethically acceptable minimum of not treating the non-combatants as mere means. The principle rules out eliminative, terror, and sadistic bombing. For they fail to meet the ethically acceptable minimum of not treating the non-combatants as mere means.

A disjunctive reading of the end-not-means principle also contrasts the types of bombing more precisely in terms of best, better, worse, and worst, as follows. First, consider the types of justifiable bombing. While similar in terms of being permissible, they differ in terms of being more and less ideal. Insofar as harmful relief bombing purposefully benefits non-combatants, it lives up to the ideal of treating others as existing for their own sakes. This recommends it. Risky tactical bombing in part falls short and in part lives up to the ideal. For while one does not undertake tactical bombing on behalf of the non-combatants, one bears the risk in risky tactical bombing for their sake. In this respect, it treats them as ends positively (to employ a term from Kant, as will be elaborated upon shortly); again, this aspect of the act commends it. Safe tactical bombing entirely falls short of the ideal of benefitting the non-combatants, not even incorporating risk in order to minimize harm. Nonetheless, like risky tactical bombing, safe tactical bombing does not violate the default (the ethically acceptable minimum requirement). For it does not use the civilians. Although it entirely falls short of the ideal, it does not fall below the ethically acceptable minimum of not treating them as mere means. Thus, safe tactical bombing may be said to treat the non-combatants as ends in terms of what it does not do; namely, it does not use them. Thus, it treats them as ends negatively (again, borrowing the term from Kant). This fact about safe tactical bombing does not provide a reason to perform the act. Rather, as noted, it establishes that reasons may be provided on its behalf since it is, in principle, a permissible act. Other things being equal, one can more easily justify harmful relief bombing than both risky and safe tactical bombing, while one can more easily justify risky than safe tactical bombing. This is to hold that harmful relief bombing could be justified in circumstances that would justify neither risky nor safe tactical bombing. For example, one could be justified in causing more harm in a case of harmful relief bombing than in a case of risky or safe tactical bombing.

Now, consider the unjustifiable cases, namely, eliminative, terror, and sadistic bombing. While similar in terms of being impermissible, they differ in terms of their wrongness. Eliminative bombing fails to treat the non-combatants as ends, even negatively. Rather, it treats them as obstacles in the way and removes them in order to achieve a goal. Accordingly, eliminative bombing violates the default of the end-not-means principle, but does so least egregiously. For it derives no further advantage from the destruction of the citizens than their being out of the way. Terror bombing, like eliminative bombing, destroys them in order to achieve victory and thereby objectionably treats them as mere means. Moreover, terror bombing is worse than eliminative bombing, as it instantiates a more complete using of the non-combatants. For terror bombing both destroys them and uses their destruction to demoralize the enemy. Nonetheless, terror bombing is not as bad as sadistic bombing. For it does not violate their status as ends as profoundly as sadistic bombing. Since one sadistically bombs solely for the sake of the terror and the harm caused to the non-combatants it stands most opposed to the ideal expressed by the end-not-means principle. For that ideal would have the non-combatants acted on behalf of, while sadistic bombing kills and terrorizes for the sake of killing and terrorizing. Thus, sadistic bombing is the worst kind of bombing.

The position that persons are ends in themselves grounds the ideal and the default of the end-not-means principle. That is, persons exist for their own sake; as existing for their own sake, one ought either to act on their behalf or, at the very least, not subordinate them to other goals. Reconsidering Bennett's reading of the principle, one realizes that while the end-not-means principle does not pick out benefiting them as the one and only way of behaving towards others as acceptable, it does rest its judgements on one ground: persons exist for their own sake. This one basis implicates a variety of ethical judgments, as the evaluation of the various types of bombing illustrate.

The disjunctive reading of the end-not-means principle compares favourably to Bennett's reading on at least two counts. First, from the truth that people are ends in themselves, the disjunctive reading generates a variety of judgements regarding the ideal, the permissible, and the impermissible. Read disjunctively, the end-not-means principle articulates common morality's intuitions that there are minimum ethically acceptable norms of behaviour and acts that rise above or fall below that standard. Moreover, read disjunctively, the principle captures nuances

concerning the better and worse amongst those acts judged
to be permissible or impermissible. The conjunctive reading
fails to capture these distinctions and nuances. Second,
although Kant's precise meaning is not at issue, the disjunctive reading captures what Kant himself proposes.

In his *Grounding for the Metaphysics of Morals*, Kant
presents the end-not-means formulation of the categorical
imperative (the moral norm that applies to us regardless of
what we want): 'So act that you use humanity, whether in
your own person or in the person of any other, always at the
same time as an end, never merely as a means' (Kant 1998,
38).[16] Shortly thereafter he notes: 'humanity might indeed
subsist if no one contributed to the happiness of others but
yet did not intentionally withdraw anything from it; but
there is still only a negative and not a positive agreement
with *humanity as an end in itself* unless everyone also tries, as
far as he can, to further the ends of others' (ibid. 39, original

[16] 'Use' here (from what is becoming the standard English scholarly
edition) is a very literal translation of Kant's *brauchst*, from the verb *brauchen*, meaning, to use, employ, or, more loosely, treat. Many translators
favour 'treat' over 'use', e.g. Thomas Kingsmill Abbott, James Ellington,
Carl J. Friedrich, and H. J. Paton (but on Paton, see below). For, in English,
one can readily be said to treat another either as an end or as a means, while
'using another as an end' sounds oxymoronic. (In German, *brauchen* applies
equally to *Zweck* (end) as to *Mittel* (means, instrument). Moreover, Kant
appears to mean it that way, as he employs it univocally to these very words in
the relevant passage.) Paton translates *brauchst* as 'treat' (Paton 1966, 91)
and, elsewhere, as 'use'. Translating the term as 'use', however, he immediately
comments, 'we are treating persons "at the same time" as an end, though we
may also be using them as a means' (Paton 1965, 165). While some reasonably choose to translate the term literally, they understandably hesitate to
speak of 'using as an end' when commenting on the text. I thank Professor
Rosemarie Deist for discussing these points with me.

emphasis). Upon articulating the end-not-means principle, Kant immediately employs the terminology of being in positive or negative agreement with it. As illustrated in the cases concerning bombing, one positively treats another as an end by advancing his welfare while one negatively treats another as an end when one does not intentionally harm him for the sake of one's goal. With such terms, Kant indicates that the end-not-means principle is to be read disjunctively.

Moreover, Kant's distinction between perfect and imperfect duties suggests the disjunctive reading. By these terms, Kant contrasts duties that oblige without exception from those that admit of exceptions. For example, to enslave another is always wrong while feeding the hungry is generally obligatory. No reasons can be offered to justify slavery; when one has no food, however, or must fulfil other conflicting and similarly weighty obligations, one may forgo feeding the hungry. Regarding persons, one grounds both perfect and imperfect duties in the end-not-means formulation of the categorical imperative. In terms of the disjunctive reading, what I term the default is our perfect duty (and treats the other as an end negatively), while the ideal is our imperfect duty (and treats the other as an end positively).

While Kant is notoriously difficult to interpret, the Kant scholar H. J. Paton asserts what amounts to the above claims. He says:

it is easy to see how this [end-not-means] principle gives rise to the distinction between perfect and imperfect duties. So far as we take the principle negatively it forbids us to use rational agents simply as a means ... This is the basis of perfect duties, and it forbids such wrongs as murder…But we must also take our principle positively: it bids us to act on the maxim of furthering the ends of rational agents. Here [regarding imperfect duties], it must be remembered, there is a place or 'play room' for discretion. (Paton 1965, 171–2)

Clearly, Paton interprets the end-not-means principle disjunctively to the effect that one ought (ideally) to treat another as an end positively and out of one's imperfect duty or (as a bare minimum for ethical behaviour) negatively and out of one's perfect duty. In short, the disjunctive reading accords with Kant's originating account. Thus, reading the end-not-means principle disjunctively both comports with Kant's account and admits of helpful distinctions and nuances absent from the conjunctive interpretation. Yet, how does this relate to the ethical relevance of the i/f distinction?

The relation between the distinction and the end-not-means principle concerns intention. By definition, one intends an end or means. Ends and means are not only the effects of agents, they are the intended effects of agents. Agents cause means for the sake of ends; using means, they cause ends for their own sake. Something is a means or an end not merely because an agent causes it, but only if the agent causes it (a means) to achieve something for the sake of which the agent acts (an end). Therefore, the end-not-means principle—not itself offering an account of intention—necessarily implies and relies on such an account. The principle relates to the ethical relevance of the i/f distinction. It does so insofar as that distinction marks the difference between objectionably relating harmfully to some person as a means and relating to some person harmfully and volitionally, but not as a means and, therefore, not necessarily objectionably. Thus, one partially locates the i/f distinction's ethical import in its relation to the moral status of persons as ends-in-themselves.

4.3.3. The distinction's moral relevance vis-à-vis the other criteria

The arguments offered thus far indicate the ethical relevance of the i/f distinction as grounded in the natures of both actions and humans. Because it receives the lion's share of attention, one might understandably think that double effect amounts to the distinction between intent and foresight. As evident from the discussion of section 1.3, however, DER requires the satisfaction of the other criteria, namely, that the act is otherwise good and proportionately grave reasons exist for acting. Given the moral relevance of the distinction, when the agent does not intend the foreseen evil and the act meets the other conditions, the act is permissible. How ought we to understand the moral relevance of the distinction in those instances in which either the act is wrongful independent of the foreseen evil or it lacks due proportion? Does the i/f distinction have moral relevance independently of these other considerations, or does it possess it only in tandem with their being satisfied? The arguments of section 4.3 establish the moral import of the i/f distinction as an independent factor that partially comprises the evaluation of certain acts. That is, other things being equal, intent of evil morally differs from foresight of the same such that the latter may be permitted in instances in which the former cannot.

Other things, however, are not always equal. Specifically, what role does the foresight of evil play in evaluating an act lacking due proportion or an otherwise wrongful act? First, consider the act lacking proportionality. Without ignorance, coercion, or extenuating circumstances, a tactical bomber destroys an insignificant military target while inflicting gross harm upon numerous non-combatants. He foresees but does not intend the harm. Does his act—which DER judges to be wrong as lacking due proportion—nonetheless morally differ from the terror bomber's? Yes and no. Yes—for considered abstractly as a kind of bombing, tactical differs from terror as what is in principle permissible differs from what is in principle not. No—for one does not consider acts only abstractly or only in principle. In the imagined concrete circumstances, this instance of tactical bombing is a morally obtuse act, displaying callous indifference to profound evil. While it is not as vicious an act as consequentially comparable terror bombing (although the vicious act would have the virtue of not being stupid), it, like terror bombing, is ruled out of bounds. The acts resemble one another in terms of being ethically out of bounds while differing in terms of why they are so.

Now consider the second question, namely, what role does the contrast between the intention and foresight of evil play in evaluating an otherwise wrongful act in which the agent foresees but does not intend some secondary evil? Imagine a police hostage-rescue unit employing a dangerous gas to disable terrorists who hold schoolchildren captive. The police know that in using the gas upon the terrorists some of the children will also be seriously harmed, but as they have no safer alternative, they use the gas. They overcome the terrorists and, as they foresaw, seriously harm some of the very children whom they sought to rescue (note the resemblance to relief bombing presented in section 4.3.2). Relying on considerations found in DER, they and many others consider their act justifiable. In contrast to this case, consider one in which some of the terrorists have been captured and imprisoned. Others decide to free them by detonating a powerful bomb against the prison wall. The terrorists know that this will seriously harm nearby residents, while not intending to do so (see the discussion at section 3.3.2 for consideration of a similar case). Indeed, they take measures to reduce the harm by destroying the wall during school hours so as not to harm children and others gone during the day. Nonetheless, they know that some people will be both present and seriously harmed. They free the prisoners, kill and harm neighbours, and are subsequently captured. In their trial for the deaths of and harm to the neighbours, the terrorists note that they did not seek to kill and harm, only to free the imprisoned. Moreover, they note that in deliberating about how to accomplish their goal, they had considered detonating the bomb while there were more people nearby, including school-aged children, as this would add to the confusion of the authorities, thereby assisting the prisoners to escape. They rejected this as targeting of the innocent. While the terrorists acknowledge full responsibility for the (wrongful) deaths and harms suffered

by the neighbours, they ask that the moral difference
between their act and that of one incorporating intentional
harm to the residents be acknowledged in their sentencing.
In their defence, they present the case of the police hostage
unit employing the gas and foreseeably harming children.

What does one make of the moral import of the i/f
distinction in cases such as the terrorists who want to
employ it to mitigate their punishment for the foreseen
evil effects of a wrongful act? The terrorists correctly claim
that targeting the neighbours as a means would have been
worse (morally) than foreseeably and coincidentally harming them. Moreover, they rightly rejected the outright intent
of harming the residents. The court of their own conscience
cannot hold them guilty of this wrong, nor may others hold
them morally guilty of this. For they did not commit the
ethically wrongful act of intentionally targeting the neighbours. (Of course, what they did was wrong.) Again, holding
that the moral import of the distinction operates independently of the other criteria, the fact that they were engaged in
an otherwise wrongful act does not eliminate the moral
difference between intent and foresight. This does not
mean, however, that the i/f distinction must be granted
legal relevance in cases of wrongful action (as the terrorists
request); nor, for that matter, in cases of right action.[17] The
terrorists can rightly claim that they did not perform the
specific act of targeting the innocent. They cannot presume,

---

[17] As will be noted in sec. 5.6, in an otherwise wrongful act, the English
law of murder allows without requiring jurors to equate foresight of an
inevitable consequence to intent. Thus, jurors could but need not find the
act of foreseeably killing the neighbours to be one of intentionally doing so.

however, that others will give this ethical fact legal import in punishing the wrongful act they did perform.

Thus, in answer to the questions bearing on the moral import of the i/f distinction in relation to the other criteria, the distinction has moral relevance independent of them (even in cases of wrongful action). It does not have such moral import, however, as to render those criteria otiose. Nor may one presume that it has legal significance (the legal import of the distinction and DER more generally will receive consideration in Chapter 5).

In conclusion, I have argued for the ethical relevance of the i/f distinction in act- and victim-focused aspects. First, I have argued that its ethical import springs from the well of ethical relevance itself, namely the ethical significance of volition. Those who deny the distinction's import thereby reject the full significance of the most basic ethical difference; namely, the difference between the voluntary and the not voluntary. Moreover, insofar as evil ought to repel us, to intend evil is wrong. The i/f distinction rightly draws the line between impermissible acts that involve intending evil and permissible acts (when complemented by the other criteria of DER) resulting in evil in which one fails to intend to avoid evil. Second, I have argued that the i/f distinction has ethical significance insofar as it reflects the unique status of persons as ends-in-themselves, a status that refers to and makes demands upon the intentions constituting acts. The i/f distinction captures how one relates to persons. When agents harm persons, they do so permissibly or impermissibly in part based upon their intentional relations to persons as ends or means. In cases of permissible harming, agents treat persons as ends, at least negatively. In cases of impermissible harming, agents treat persons as mere means, failing to treat them as ends even negatively. Thus, the i/f distinction and DER are ethically reasonable, indeed, required for a consistent, sound ethic.

These arguments establish DER's most controverted claim; namely, that the i/f distinction has ethical significance. Nonetheless, a number of issues remain (for example, the above-noted reception of DER in the law), which I address in the fifth and final chapter.

5

DER and remaining considerations

DER stands on firm philosophical ground. The i/f distinction applies in the customarily contrasted cases and has ethical relevance. These positions concern ethics and the debate surrounding double effect. Before concluding, a number of typically neglected questions deserve attention. When DER justifies one's act, does one owe reparations for causing foreseen harm? How does double effect apply in cases of allowing? Can one employ double effect to evaluate one's otherwise good act that becomes problematic due to another's wrongful conduct? For example, may a merchant who foresees that some customers will abuse an otherwise legitimate product still sell it? How does double effect relate to the law? Given double effect's bearing upon basic norms such as that concerning killing, the law and public policy will have something to say about acts justified in accordance with such reasoning. For, while an individual may rely on DER to justify his action as ethical, he cannot thereby presume its legality. An act may be moral yet illegal or vice versa (for example, under-age drinking or adultery). Moreover, while the i/f distinction has independent ethical

relevance, must the law accord it similar independent
legal import (as mooted in section 4.3)? Accordingly, the
relation between DER, its elements, and the law arises.
Moreover, insofar as DER arises from the thought of certain
of its moral theologians, how does the Roman Catholic
Church receive DER? I now address these remaining
questions.

5.1.   DER AND REPARATIONS

DER justifies one's acting notwithstanding one's harming
those not deserving harm. While one harms, one does no
wrong; one acts permissibly (if, of course, one satisfies the
criteria noted in section 1.3). One injures without doing
injustice. Nonetheless, such injury calls for repair. Double-
effect cases will often require one to make reparations to the
victim. In the hysterectomy and terminal sedation cases this
does not have relevance, for in both cases the victim dies.
Moreover, in terminal sedation the act benefits the very one
who dies and in hysterectomy it benefits the mother, the
person most interested in the welfare of the foetus. In the
case of tactical bombing, however, maimed victims can be
helped. Moreover, the relatives of dead non-combatants
will be harmed in their loss, for example, of a provider.
Here one finds injuries for which one has full responsibility.
Clearly, while justice does not prohibit one's act, because of
one's complete responsibility, it does require repair. Having

evaluated such an act as permissible, one now obligatorily assists those whom one has harmed.[1]

Yet, who owes reparations? Does the tactical bomber himself? No. For he acts as an agent of his country. Presuming (as stipulated) that his country wages a just war for the sake of a just peace, it will be the responsibility of his country and others answerable for establishing a just peace to compensate non-combatant victims. This includes the victors, the vanquished, and those benefiting from the consequent peace who can assist the harmed. For to the extent to which a just peace requires amends for those harmful acts ordered towards peace, those responsible for and benefited by a peaceful outcome rightly bear these costs. The same holds more generally of acts justified by DER that require reparations.

5.2.   DER AND ALLOWING

One point mooted in section 1.2 concerns DER's application to cases of intentionally or foreseeably allowing evil. The classic uses of DER do not include instances of allowing evil, being exclusively cases of causing harm. Of course, this is in keeping with allowings more generally receiving less attention than causings. Moreover, as intent does not

---

[1] As Mr Ashley Puzzo has brought to my attention, reparations for injury do not figure in the justification of the act that injures. That is, one justifies the act in terms of the harm prior to, not after reparations. Reparations follow from the agent's acknowledgment of full responsibility for the harm.

characteristically attend what one allows, the contrast between intent and foresight drawn by double effect does not arise in typical cases of allowing. In any case, one may apply DER to contrast impermissible from permissible instances of intentionally or foreseeably allowing evil. Before doing so, allowing itself requires clarification.

What is it to allow? Briefly (for the topic of allowing itself constitutes a monograph-length study), a cause is that from which or on account of which some effect is or is the way it is. Allowing feeds parasitically on causing. To allow requires that there be some cause other than oneself. Moreover, one must be able to prevent the cause from bringing about its effect. Thus, allowing has two concepts prior to it: causing and preventing. When one can and knowingly and without coercion one does not prevent the cause from bringing about its effect, one allows the effect. The current causes a leaf to float down the stream; I could but do not prevent the leaf: I allow the leaf to float downstream.

One notes a number of characteristics of allowings, so defined. First, unlike what one causes, which actuality (what one does) establishes, unrealized possibility defines what one allows (what one could but does not do). Accordingly, what one allows has an indeterminacy and relativeness in contrast to the determinacy and independent character of what one causes. Thus, one causes very few things in comparison to what one allows. The countless number of things one allows, however, must always be considered in relation to the possibilities they exclude. On this latter point, when I can prevent only one leaf at a time from floating down the stream, then at any given time, I allow the many leaves to float down the stream only insofar as I could prevent any one of them, but not all of them together. That is, at any given time, I allow only one leaf of the many to float down the stream. Thus, when speaking of allowings, one must take care not to aggregate all that one allows. For one cannot prevent all that one allows, only some of what one allows. Accordingly, allowing can only have a relative sense.

Finally, one notes that allowing is not immediately opposed to causing or doing. Rather, it contrasts with preventing. Since most preventings involve doing or causing, most allowings oppose causings. This, however, need not be the case. I might, for example, stop preventing something by a doing and thereby be said to allow it. For example, if I prevent the boat from sinking by plugging the hole with my hand and I stop preventing it from sinking by removing my hand, I allow the boat to sink by removing my hand. In this instance my doing is a stopping of my prevention and, thereby, an allowing.[2] With this conception of allowing in mind, consider DER and cases of allowing harm.

Quinn proposes two such cases, the Guinea Pig Case (GP) and the Direction of Resources Case (DR). As Quinn describes the cases, there is a:

shortage of resources for the investigation and proper treatment of a new, life-threatening disease. [In DR] doctors decide to cope by selectively treating only those who can be cured most easily, leaving the more stubborn cases untreated. In [GP], doctors

---

[2] Thus, acts such as removing a patient from a ventilator count as allowings (in this instance, an allowing to die). For in such acts one stops preventing and, thereby, allows.

decide on a crash experimental program in which they deliberately leave the stubborn cases untreated in order to learn more about the nature of the disease. By this strategy they reasonably expect to do as much long-term medical good as they would in DR.... In neither case do the nontreated know about or consent to the decision against treating them. (Quinn 1989, 336)

Considering DR and GP, two points are in order. First, doctors act wrongly in both DR and GP to the extent to which they do not inform the patients nor do the patients consent to non-treatment. Thus, in both cases the doctors wrongly deceive their patients. Second, in both DR and GP the doctors presumably do care for and do treat the patients, they just do not use the scarce resources on them. That is, they manage the patients's symptoms and provide standard care while not attempting to cure them. (Of course, given their deception, the patients think that they do receive curative treatment for the disease.) Thus, the question posed to DER concerns whether one may contrast these two (already wrongful because deceitful) acts such that GP is worse than DR because it is an intentional in contrast to a foreseeable allowing. No—for, were the doctors to inform the patients that they will not receive the scarce resource because they are amongst the least likely to benefit and were the patients to consent to being studied to see the progression of the disease, there would be nothing objectionable to DR or GP. For, given the scarcity of the resource, some patients will be allowed to develop, and die from, the life-threatening disease. DER does not have a role to play in evaluating DR and GP as Quinn presents them. For what is at issue is not a contrast between intending what one allows in contrast to foreseeing what one allows, as would need to be the case to employ DER. Rather, in DR and GP one encounters two legitimate allowings but for the deceit and subsequent non-consent involved in both of them. Perhaps the difficulty of finding appropriate examples of allowing by which to test DER itself illustrates the rarity of resorting to double effect to justify a case of foreseeably allowing what one may not intentionally allow.

In any case, it seems that with relevant revisions DR and GP might serve. Let us say that in administering a scarce miracle drug, doctors reasonably choose to give it to the most treatable patients. There is not enough of the drug, however, for all of the most treatable patients. Thus, regardless of what the doctors do, some of those most likely to benefit from the drug will be allowed to develop the disease. Because the doctors will care for those patients not receiving the drug as they develop the disease, knowledge of how the disease progresses will be gained. It would prove beneficial, however, to compare the drug's efficacy to that of a placebo (in order to isolate the drug's effects from other factors influencing the outcome). This knowledge will assist in developing future therapies. Additionally, amongst the most treatable patients there is a cohort in which the development of the disease would be most advantageous to study. The doctors realize that if they were to choose patients from this cohort to receive the placebo, they would derive more useful knowledge than a random assignment of patients to receive the placebo would generate. Nevertheless, the doctors decide to conduct a trial of the miracle drug amongst the most treatable patients, randomly assigning patients to receive the placebo. Knowing that some of them will receive the drug while others will receive a placebo, the patients consent. Call this case (in which doctors randomly choose patients to receive the placebo) DR*. Up to this point, there is no need to employ DER to evaluate the contemplated allowings in DR*. For the doctors reasonably intend to use the scarce drug only within the population of those whom it will most likely benefit while studying the disease amongst those randomly receiving the placebo (which group will, likely, also include some of the noted cohort).

In contrast to DR*, consider GP*. In GP* the doctors intend to allow the disease to develop in the cohort in which the progression of the disease would be most advantageous to study, exclusively choosing members of this group to receive the placebo. The doctors do not deceive any of the patients. For neither the doctors nor the patients know who belongs to the cohort prior to the study. The patients consent to receive the placebo if they fall within the relevant group. It is permissible randomly to allow the disease to develop in patients belonging to this cohort, as will occur in DR* (given that it is likely some of them will end up receiving the placebo). Yet, may one intend to allow it to develop in the cohort? That is, is it ethical deliberately not to choose members of the cohort for drug-treatment and, thereby, to intend to allow them to develop the disease? Here, DER has a role to play. For here one contrasts intent and foresight.

Employing DER, one holds that DR* is while GP* is not permissible, insofar as in GP* the doctors intend to allow the terminal disease to harm the patients in the cohort as a means of advancing their knowledge of the disease. Of course, in DR* the doctors know that they will also learn useful information about the disease from the members of the cohort randomly assigned to receive the placebo. Nonetheless, they do not choose not to give the drug to members of the cohort in order to learn more about the disease. Recalling the discussion of section 4.3, one may criticize GP* on two ethically important counts. First, it instances the use of persons by seeking to allow the disease to develop in some of them rather than others insofar as that is more useful. Second, it incorporates malevolence in a plan to allow grievous harm to certain patients rather than others. DR* need not suffer these moral defects. Thus, DER permits DR* while prohibiting GP*. Such cases illustrate how DER applies to allowings.

To rectify a case of intentional allowing what does DER ask of the agent? If one may foreseeably allow the outcome, then one need not prevent the outcome. For example, since DR* is justified, the agent in GP* who acknowledges the wrongness of his intentional allowing need not prevent the disease from developing in all those of the cohort in whom he intentionally allowed it to develop. (Indeed, we must keep in mind the caveat noted above concerning not aggregating what one allows; as stipulated, he simply cannot prevent it from developing in all of them.) He need simply no longer intend to allow it to develop in members of that group. That is, he must no longer choose not to administer the drug to them so as to allow the disease to develop in them. Randomly assigning patients to receive the drug will presumably result in more of the cohort being cured than would occur were they chosen not to receive the drug. (Thus, at least in this case, changing one's intent actually changes what occurs even in an instance of allowing.)

Further questions arise concerning DER and allowing. First, common morality typically holds a greater moral presumption against causing harm than against allowing it. Does this result in DER's requiring less of a justification for foreseeably allowing than for foreseeably causing harm? For example, in employing DER may one allow greater harm than one may cause? Second, does this mean that it is typically worse intentionally to cause than intentionally to allow consequentially comparable harm? Of course, a complete response would take one far afield of DER, into perhaps even more controverted claims concerning the do/allow distinction (or distinctions): what it is, how one makes it, and what ethical relevance, if any, it has. Such questions easily comprise their own book-length study.

To answer these two questions as they relate to DER, examples prove helpful. In contrast to DR* and GP*, consider two cases in which one treats terminally ill patients with a drug that itself causes another terminal disease in those receiving it. The patients are much better off receiving the drug than not. In Prolong, physicians administer the drug in order to prolong patients's lives, foreseeing that this will also cause the patients to develop a distinct terminal illness from which they will die later than they otherwise would have. In Research, physicians administer the same drug in order to study the new terminal illness. DER permits Prolong but not Research and DR* but not GP*. How does the permission of DR* (a foreseen allowing) compare with that of Prolong (a foreseen causing)? If the response to the permissible cases were to differ, it would be found in the due-proportion criterion treated in section 1.3. That is, if there is always a greater presumption against causing harm than there is against allowing it, one would have to offer more good consequences in Prolong than one would have to offer in Direction of Resources*. Comparing these limited cases, however, it seems that this is not at issue and that whatever distinction common morality makes between causing and allowing harm, it does not exert influence here. For what justifies acting in the doing of harm found in Prolong also justifies acting in the allowing of harm in DR*; namely, that there is little else one could do. For in Prolong, one either cures one terminal illness and causes another, or one allows the patient to die of the current terminal illness now. In DR*, because of the drug's scarcity, for every patient one cures one also allows another to die from the disease. (Of course, this is not to assert that typical causings do not differ from typical allowings of harm. That, however, is another topic.) Indeed, these cases do not seem to require DER to justify them except when contrasted with objectionable cases like Research and GP*. For what else would one do when faced with the question of efficiently using a scarce resource (as in DR*) but try to achieve the greatest good? One does not first recur to DER in such a case as one does in, say, tactical bombing. For in tactical bombing one presumably has myriad reasonable choices (to bomb, not to bomb, to bomb other targets, and so on), while in DR*, one's reasonable choices are so constrained that using the resource most efficiently requires little further justification, until one imagines an objectionable case like GP*. Thus, we might think of cases like DR* and Prolong as requiring DER for purposes of contrast with unjustifiable cases. That is, basic practical reasonableness justifies one in scarce-resource cases such as DR*. Imagining GP*, one employs DER to contrast it with the otherwise justified case of DR*. Tactical bombing, hysterectomy, and terminal sedation, however, require DER for justification (and not simply as they stand in contrast to other, objectionable cases, for example, terror bombing). For in such cases practical reasonableness does not immediately apprehend such acts as what one ought to do. In answer to the first question, in light of these cases, DER itself does not contrast foreseeable allowing with foreseeable causing of harm such that the former always requires less of a justification than the latter.

To return to the second question, is it always worse intentionally to cause than intentionally to allow consequentially comparable harm? For example, does the moral import of intention coupled with that of the do/allow distinction differentiate between Research and GP*? It seems not. The intentional doing in Research is no worse than the intentional allowing in GP*. This, however, may be in part because in Research the disease will be caused by a drug that heals the patients from another illness. One would permissibly give them this drug absent the wrongful intent of causing the disease. Again, in GP* one would permissibly allow the disease to develop in members of the cohort absent the wrongful intent of ensuring that they suffer it. Alternative contrasting cases would surely result in different conclusions.

In any case, to return to the issue of allowings, DER certainly applies to them. Notably, one's commitment to DER makes more of a difference in cases of doing than in cases of allowing. For when an agent takes DER seriously, he may, amongst other things, change what he intends. When he changes what he intends this more likely changes what occurs when he does something than when he allows something. This may in part be due to the indeterminate and relative character of allowing. For, as noted above in considering what it is to allow, one cannot aggregate one's allowings. Thus, when one no longer intends to allow, one need not thereby prevent. One may, as in the case of the doctor who abandons his intent to allow in GP* to foreseeably allowing in DR*, continue to allow without intent. This holds true even when one must do something in order to allow—cases of stopping one's prevention. So, for example, I may stop preventing the boat from sinking by removing my finger from the hole I plug. In doing so, I may intend to allow the boat to sink, but I need not. When I change my objectionable intent to allow the boat to sink (say, in order to recoup insurance money), I may still remove my finger (allow the boat to sink). For I may remove it because I have something better to do (say, rescue someone drowning). Thus, when agents follow it, the prohibition against intentionally allowing bad things to happen need not result in fewer bad things happening while the prohibition against intending to cause bad things will typically reduce the number of bad things that happen. This is interesting, albeit not surprising. For in speaking of what we ought not to intend to allow, DER does not thereby typically change what we allow. In speaking about what we ought not intentionally to cause, however, it does typically influence what we cause, insofar as intent partially constitutes many of our causings (those that we most precisely speak of as actions). Before concluding our ethical considerations, I turn to double effect's analysis of one's otherwise good act as it foreseeably furthers another's wrongful act.

5.3. DER AND THE WRONGFUL ACTS OF OTHER AGENTS

The cases thus far considered address one's own acts exclusively. As noted in section 1.1 (in the case of passive scandal whereby one's own otherwise acceptable deed foreseeably contributed to another's wrongful act and spiritual downfall), double effect applies to cases in which one foresees another's abuse of one's otherwise good act. For example, a person who gives money to a panhandler who may spend it on alcohol would reasonably analyse her act in terms of double effect. She seeks to help the beggar, she foresees the risk of his using the money badly, but does not intend that he do so, and the good of helping an apparently honest beggar outweighs the bad of enabling him to become drunk, if he turns out to be deceitful. Of course, the due-care requirement asks her to avoid risking his becoming drunk. Perhaps she could give food or food-vouchers rather than money, thereby ensuring that he would be fed. Absent viable alternatives, however, she acts well although she thereby risks his inebriation. Were he to become drunk in part due to her generous act, she could show its justifiability and reasonableness in terms of DER. Of course, the fact that her act was one of risking differentiates this case from those in which one knows with certainty that others will abuse one's otherwise good act. Let us address such cases.

Consider manufacturers and merchants who make and sell such ordinary products as spray-paint and glue, knowing that some will abuse the same. They may assess their acts in terms of double effect. It would seem that the due-care requirement here looms large. How diligently have these individuals attempted to avoid lending their products to abuse, or selling them to those who would abuse them? This question becomes more pronounced when one considers that regardless of whether consumers use or abuse an otherwise legitimate product, those who make and sell that product realize a profit. Given the inherent conflict of interest that such cases pose, those who would resort to double effect to justify the production and sale of such products must do so with scrupulous attention to due care. For example (abstracting from the particulars of an actual case), in South America thousands of children resort to glue-sniffing to escape the despair of their grim prospects. They often sniff glue employed in the manufacture and repair of shoes. The manufacturers and merchants of that glue might resort to double effect, holding that they act ethically, providing a necessity, and that they foresee but do not intend the profound harm the children suffer. When one considers due care, however, one sees that these manufacturers and merchants fail to exercise it diligently. For example, some glue manufacturers introduce the noxious oil of mustard seed to deter glue-sniffing. While this places a modest burden upon those who make and repair shoes (prior to drying, the modified glue has a pungent smell) it does not affect the usefulness of the glue. The manufacturers of the altered glue, merchants who sell it, and those who use it find this a safe, effective, economical, and ethical means of lowering abuse. The acts of those who take such measures comply with the due-care criterion of double effect. Those, however, who do not take steps to reduce or eliminate the abuse of their product fail to exercise due diligence to avoid this evil. Indeed, noting that those who add mustard-seed oil to their glue also see their sales diminish (in part due to the decreased abuse of it) one reasonably wonders whether those who do not do so display a callous indifference to the harm affiliated with their product and a willingness to profit from such abuse. DER does not justify such an act.

In scientific research and development, one constantly faces the double-edged character of technology ordered towards a good end by its inventors who foresee that others will use it badly. High-definition copiers made for business will be used in counterfeiting. Research on contagious viruses for the purpose of developing vaccines will be used for biological weapons. Tests to identify those subject to genetic disease so that they may be cared for will be used to discriminate against the same. Without multiplying examples, DER allows one to analyse the morality of developing new technologies for the good when one foresees that others will use them badly.

To develop the lineaments of double effect's application to the many instances in which technology facilitates wrongful actions, consider how mundane and ubiquitous office-copiers and printers can be employed by counterfeiters (and are regularly). Here again, due care deserves and has received significant attention. Indeed, aware that governments might prohibit or significantly restrict the distribution of their products, manufacturers go to great lengths to render their technology inhospitable to counterfeiting (while realizing that they cannot eliminate that abuse). Thus, makers of printers and copiers typically design them to mark documents so that legal authorities may trace documents back to the machine that produced them. This reduces, while not eradicating, abuse of this technology. In light of DER, one would consider the production of such generally beneficial technologies permissible, particularly given the due care exercised by manufacturers.

Clearly, double effect has many insights to offer when employed to analyse the ethics of acting given another's abuse of one's otherwise good act. Having addressed this and other ethical issues, I now consider DER's reception in international law bearing upon war.

5.4.   DOUBLE EFFECT, NON-COMBATANT CASUALTIES, AND THE LAWS OF WAR

In the theory of just war that may be traced back to Cicero via Augustine and Aquinas, one finds criteria to evaluate going to war (*jus ad bellum*) and criteria to evaluate conduct in war (*jus in bello*). A war must be just in order for one to act justly in any specific act by which one prosecutes it. Of course, while the injustice of a war vitiates the justice of any act by which one pursues it, the justice of a war does not establish the justice of acts comprising it. One could act unjustly in an otherwise just war. For example, in the fire-bombing of Dresden the Allied forces unjustly conducted a just war by targeting non-combatants in order to terrorize the German populace. Similarly, the United States acted unjustly in bombing the civilian populations of Hiroshima and Naga-saki. These historic acts of terror bombing exemplify unjust conduct in a just war. Thus, for one's conduct of war to be just, both the war and the individual act must be just.

In evaluating the justice of conduct in war, thinkers advance two principles: proportionality and discrimination. As it bears upon the conduct of war, proportionality com-pares, for example, the military good one seeks to secure to the harm that one will thereby cause. The principle of proportionality limits the amount of force one may employ to achieve a military objective. Discrimination concerns in what respect and against whom one may employ force. It bears upon weapons, tactics, and targets.

One finds the principle of discrimination (and, thereby, DER, as will become evident) codified in international law. For example, while most of the 1907 Hague Convention concerns the conduct of war vis-à-vis combatants, one discerns the prohibition of attacking non-combatants in Convention IV, Article 25, which states that 'the attack or bombardment, by whatever means, of towns, villages, dwellings, or buildings which are undefended is prohibited' (Roberts and Guelff 2000, 78). With respect to aerial bombardment, Article 22 of the 1923 Hague Draft Rules of Aerial Warfare holds that 'aerial bombardment for the purpose of terrorizing the civilian population, of destroying or damaging private property not of military character, or of injuring non-combatants is prohibited' (ibid. 144). (While not a formally binding agreement, the 1923 Hague Draft Rules exemplify broadly accepted laws of war as they bear upon air warfare.) While ruling out terror bombing, in Article 24 the draft rules permit aerial bombardment when 'directed exclusively at... military forces; military works; military establishments or depots; factories constituting important and well-known centres engaged in the manufacture of arms, ammunition or distinctively military supplies...' (ibid. 145). In paragraph 4 of Article 24, the draft rules hold that:

In the immediate neighborhood of the operations of land forces, the bombardment of cities, towns, villages, dwellings or buildings is legitimate provided that there exists a reasonable presumption that the military concentration is sufficiently important to justify such bombardment, having regard to the danger thus caused to the civilian population. (Ibid. 145)

One reasonably interprets the 1923 Hague Draft Rules as codifications of the criteria DER employs in distinguishing between terror and tactical bombing.

Putting aside these specific cases of aerial bombardment, one finds double-effect criteria codified in the 1977 Geneva Protocol I, Article 51, paragraph 2, which states that 'the civilian population as such, as well as individual civilians, shall not be the object of attack. Acts or threats of violence the primary purpose of which is to spread terror among the civilian population are prohibited' (ibid. 448). Again, in Article 57, paragraph 2, the Protocol implies the permissibility of foreseen civilian casualties when due care is exercised, saying:

Those who plan or decide upon an attack shall: (ii) take all feasible precautions in the choice of means and methods of attack with a view to avoiding, and in any event minimizing, incidental loss of civilian life, injury to civilians and damage to civilian objects; (iii) refrain from deciding to launch any attack which may be expected to cause incidental loss of civilian life, injury to civilians, damage to civilian objects, or a combination thereof, which would be excessive in relation to the concrete and direct military advantage anticipated. (Ibid. 452–3)

Clearly, the Protocol here instantiates the very criteria of due care and proportionality one finds in DER.

In their judgements concerning illegitimate targeting of non-combatants and legitimate military acts that incidentally harm non-combatants, DER and international law agree. International laws of war accept, indeed codify, the judgements of double effect as they bear on the conduct of war. In this important arena one sees that international law and policy agree with DER.

5.5.   DOUBLE EFFECT AND PUBLIC POLICY CONCERNING EUTHANASIA

The debate contrasting the legally accepted practice of terminal sedation with the generally prohibited acts of physician-assisted suicide (PAS) and voluntary euthanasia reveals another point of contact between DER, law, and public policy. Briefly, one defines PAS as a physician's prescribing a lethal drug at the request of a competent, terminally ill patient so that she may kill herself. Voluntary euthanasia refers to a physician's administering a lethal injection at the request of a competent, terminally ill patient in order to kill her. In many countries, law and policy permit terminal sedation (and other acts that lead to a patient's death, for example, the withdrawal of ventilators at the end of life) while rejecting the legality of PAS and euthanasia.[3] Advocates for the legalization of PAS and euthanasia argue that law and public policy err in distinguishing between these consequentially similar acts. Proponents of PAS and euthanasia often quarrel with the use of double effect in contrasting these acts with currently accepted practices such as terminal sedation. A number of questions arise concerning the use of DER in law and public policy.

Insofar as DER comes out of a religious tradition, is it fit for use in increasingly pluralistic and secular societies? As noted in Chapter 1, DER originates in the work of Thomas Aquinas, a Catholic saint, theologian, and philosopher of the 1200s. Nonetheless, double-effect reasoning is not a religious doctrine. The acknowledged intuitive support given double effect by common morality, its internationally accepted use in the just conduct of war, and the weight given

---

[3] Currently, euthanasia is legal in the Netherlands and Belgium. PAS is legal in the Netherlands, Belgium, Switzerland, and the US state of Oregon. Nations and jurisdictions that prohibit PAS and euthanasia typically permit terminal sedation and other acts that foreseeably lead to the patient's death.

to double effect by contemporary secular philosophers such as Nagel and Quinn indicate its non-religious character. It is simply a non-consequentialist way of thinking about hard cases.

More to the point, is it reasonable to employ double effect while at the same time accepting a patient's refusal of medical interventions that incorporates the patient's intent to die? Call such a refusal a suicidal refusal in contrast to that of a patient not intent upon securing his death, but who simply finds the medical intervention too burdensome. When one acquiesces in a suicidal refusal, may one consistently oppose other suicidal or homicidal acts such as PAS and euthanasia? Yes. To honour a patient's suicidal refusal of a medical intervention does not mean that one would be inconsistent in rejecting PAS and euthanasia. For, even when a suicidal patient seeks to ensure her death by refusing medical intervention and her physician and society honour her refusal, her refusal need not be accepted as a suicide. It need be accepted solely as a refusal of medical intervention. Societies reasonably acquiesce in a patient's suicidal refusal of medical intervention while opposing the intentional killing of a patient or intentional assistance in suicide. For they accept the suicidal *refusal*, not the *suicidal* refusal of medical intervention. Those who would argue (as advocates of PAS and euthanasia do) that one cannot consistently honour suicidal refusals while rejecting other acts that incorporate the intent to die fail to see that one accepts refusals of medical interventions simply as refusals.

Moreover, the refusal (suicidal or otherwise) that leads to death can be differentiated from PAS in terms of the physician–patient relationship. Specifically, if a patient were not to have the legal right to refuse medical intervention and a physician were not to have the legal obligation to honour this refusal, what would be the alternative way of working out the physician–patient relationship? The alternative would be that the physician would have the right to mandate medical intervention and the patient the obligation to accept it. This, however, is not tolerable. For human beings are uniquely suited to live in accordance with their own apprehension of what is good; that is, human beings are appropriately self-ruled. A society that would require a patient to undertake the medical interventions proposed by his physician would act against the nature of the human subject by subordinating him to the will of another, identifiable individual.

On the other hand, to refuse to entitle patients to the assistance of physicians in suicide limits only the means patients may employ to achieve their goals. It does not thereby subordinate them to any other individual's will; indeed, it does not broadly prevent them from committing suicide. Rather, it prevents them from doing so with the assistance of a physician. Those who would argue that the legal right to refuse medical intervention cannot consist-ently be accepted without thereby accepting the legality of PAS and euthanasia fail to reflect sufficiently on the alternative to legalizing the right to refuse. Thus, one can without inconsistency accept the right to refuse medical interventions while rejecting the legitimacy of PAS and voluntary active euthanasia. Nonetheless, other objections to accommodating DER in law and public policy bearing on the end-of-life come to mind.

For example, can the distinction between intent and foresight be drawn in the clinical setting? Recalling Cajetan's (sixteenth-century) illustration of the distinction by the case of the doctor and the foreseen bad side effects of the medicine he prescribes (noted in section 1.2), the distinction seems particularly well suited to medical practice. For example, does an oncologist want to cause the pain and suffering she knows she will cause to her patient (by prescribing chemotherapy) or does she not want it at all, but rather wants to kill the cancer and knows she will cause pain and suffering while curing her patient? Here one must avoid confusing intent with an affective or emotional response to some outcome. When one is relieved at the death of one's patient, did one intend the patient's death? To think so is to conflate intent with emotion. As noted in section 3.4.1, one may be affectively relieved or glad at some outcome that one did not intend at all. Moreover, one can be affectively grieved or unhappy at an intended means or end achieved. For example, one may regret a successfully performed amputation; yet, this does not establish that one did not intend the amputation. Of course, a physician may be relieved when a patient dies whose last days were full of suffering. Does this mean that he cannot be sure that in prescribing an analgesic he intended to relieve pain and did not intend to kill? No more so than an oncologist who is pleased to see his patient's hair falling out (because he knows it means the chemotherapy functions) cannot be sure that he did not seek to make his patient's hair fall out. Intention to kill or to assist a patient's suicide and relief at the death of a patient whom one has not intentionally killed differ as a cause differs from an effect, or as action differs from reaction. Here there is opacity and ambiguity, but it does not obscure intent. Relief at a patient's death is an affective or emotional response, not revelatory of intent that is an effective, causal desire. Thus, clinical acts admit, indeed call for, the distinction between intent and foresight.

To consider yet another objection, ought one to contrast terminal sedation as a foreseen but not intended death on the one hand with both PAS and euthanasia as intended deaths on the other? Do not PAS and euthanasia themselves differ in terms of the relevant agents's intentions of the patient's death? They do. In both acts, however, agents do intend the patient's death. This is straightforwardly the case in euthanasia, for in euthanasia the physician intends to kill the patient and the patient intends to be killed. In PAS the physician has the intent to help the patient kill himself. Correspondingly, the patient has the intent to kill himself as so enabled. These intents differ from those present in euthanasia while still being ordered towards the patient's death. The patient intends to be the proximate cause of his own death while the physician intends to assist the patient to be so. One notes that some might be tempted to argue that in PAS the physician need only intend to prescribe a lethal drug. He need not intend that the patient fill the prescription, nor need he intend that the patient ingest the lethal drug. Similarly, following this line of reasoning, the patient need not intend to fill the prescription, nor need he intend to take the drug were he to fill it. He need only intend to receive a prescription for a lethal drug. This approach errs, however, in thinking that one understands the intents present in an act of PAS by considering an unrealized instance of the same. An act, however, as its very name suggests, is something realized, actual. Bearing this in mind, in PAS the physician and the patient intend that the patient die upon ingesting the drug. Thus, while PAS and euthanasia themselves differ, they both incorporate intentions that the patient die (either at the hands of the physician or at his own hands with the physician's help). Thus, PAS and euthanasia incorporate lethal intent and contrast with terminal sedation (and other practices such as honouring a patient's refusal or withdrawal of life-prolonging medical interventions) where lethal intent is absent.

Conceding the above, is DER not out of step with legal accounts of responsibility for the consequences of one's act, regardless of one's intent? From a legal standpoint, terminal sedation is an act of killing; other practices (honouring a patient's refusal or withdrawal of life-prolonging medical interventions) also legally implicate one in the patient's subsequent death. Does recourse to DER not deny these accounts of legal responsibility? No. For double effect does not distinguish degrees of responsibility (as noted in section 4.1.2). Rather, it contrasts different acts for which agents have full responsibility. The criteria in terms of which one has full responsibility for some outcome differ from those in terms of which one establishes that for which one has full responsibility. Double effect concerns the criteria establishing that for which one has full responsibility. It holds that in terminal sedation one is entirely responsible for the death of the patient insofar as one knowingly and willingly caused it, but not responsible for it as intended. So, one is responsible for a death, but not for active euthanasia that is, by definition, intended. Thus, as applied to terminal sedation (and, *mutatis mutandis,* to the above-noted cases) double effect agrees with law and public policy and serves as a sound basis for both.

5.6.   DOUBLE EFFECT AS APPLIED TO WRONGFUL ACTS AND THE LAW

Now consider the question mooted in section 4.3.3 concerning how the law ought to regard the i/f distinction in the case of a wrongful act in which the agent foresees but does not intend some secondary evil. Recall the case introduced there. Some terrorists decide to free their captured comrades by detonating a bomb beside a prison wall. They do not intend it to kill nearby residents, but know that it will. Indeed, they take measures to reduce the harm to neighbours by destroying the wall during the day. They free the prisoners, kill nearby residents, and are subsequently captured. In their trial, the terrorists argue that they did not seek to kill (even as a means), only to free. They note that in deliberating about how to accomplish their goal, they had considered detonating the bomb while more people were present, thereby adding to the confusion of the authorities and assisting escape. They rejected this as targeting of the innocent. The terrorists acknowledge full responsibility for the (still wrongful) deaths and harms suffered by the neighbours, while asking that they not be held responsible for murdering (intentionally killing) the residents.

What ought the law to make of the moral import of the i/f distinction in such a case? The terrorists correctly claim that targeting the neighbours as a means would have been morally worse than the wrongful act they performed. Must the law grant this ethical point legal relevance in cases of wrongful action? As a point of fact, one notes that the law does not entirely accord this moral difference legal weight. For example, in the English law of murder, when death is foreseen as an inevitable consequence of a wrongful act, this fact can count as evidence that it was intended, and, therefore, constitutes murder. Of course, the fact that jurors can but need not conclude that an otherwise bad actor also intended a secondary evil gives the moral difference between intent and foresight some legal import. In such a system of law, the wrongful act incorporating foresight of evil is possibly although not necessarily judged less harshly than that incorporating intent of the same. This is one way for the law to acknowledge that it differs from ethics while according ethically significant differences some legal import. It is reasonable. For as an artefact partially based upon ethics, the law is tasked with goals such as deterrence and retribution not salient in morality. More to the point, in this instance, the law must determine what counts as evidence of intent. The English law of murder allows jurors the discretion of granting the distinction legal weight. Presumably they will do so in light of considerations that come easily to mind (for example, the risks the agents bore to avoid the foreseen harm, the due care they may have exercised to mitigate it, the egregiousness of the evil, and so on). Yet, they need not accord these features legal significance, nor does that seem a flaw, given the noted tasks born by the law. For example, that agents cannot presume that the most charitable interpretation of their wrongful acts will be granted them by the law may act as a deterrent to acting badly. As deterrence is one function of law, it serves as a reasonable basis upon which the law may choose not to grant the i/f distinction full legal relevance. Thus, in answer to the question of how the law ought to regard the i/f distinction in the case of a wrongful act, it ought to do so in light of the law's purposes.

I have noted the law's reception of double effect in military and medical arenas (and of its most famous element, the i/f distinction). One might speak of these relations as 'double effect *and* the law'. There is another, largely ignored, nonetheless intriguing, relation that one might speak of as 'double effect *in* the law'. I now briefly consider that relation and the ways in which it parallels ethic's reliance on double effect to deal with certain hard cases.

5.7. DER IN LAW

As noted in the introduction, double effect results when an ethic incorporating exceptionless norms confronts hard cases where one attempts to pursue good and avoid evil. Constitutions often incorporate bills of rights that enumerate what one may think of as exceptionless legal norms. For example, the US Constitution's Bill of Rights begins with the monitory 'congress shall make no law...'. This is an exceptionless prohibition that prevents the legislature from making laws that, amongst other things, establish or inhibit the free exercise of religion. Given such absolute legal norms, it is reasonable to expect that law will have its own hard cases in which legislators cannot achieve some communal good without impeding another. In fact, this is the situation one finds. Thus, for example, constitutional scholars and judges confront hard legal cases. They do so because they admit exceptionless legal norms—as the legal scholar Edward Lyons notes (Lyons 2005, 508–43). This legal situation resembles the quandary faced in ethics. Interestingly, the resources developed in the law resemble DER, as a brief consideration of certain court decisions indicates.

For example, one US Supreme Court Case (entitled *Smith*) concerns Smith and Black who were fired by a private drug rehabilitation centre because of their use of peyote (an illegal hallucinogenic drug) in rites of their Native American Church.[4] They were denied state unemployment compensation under a law disqualifying those discharged for work-related misconduct. They sued, holding that their right freely to exercise their religion was violated by the law prohibiting sacramental peyote use and resulting in their denial of unemployment benefits. The Court ruled that 'the Free Exercise Clause permits the State to prohibit sacramental peyote use and thus to deny unemployment benefits to persons discharged for such use' (*Smith*, syllabus). The Court distinguished between laws directed towards

[4] The full title of the case is *Employment Div., Ore. Dept. of Human Res. v. Smith, 494 U.S. 872* (1990).

restricting the free exercise of religion and laws that have the effect of restricting religion, asserting:

> although a State would be 'prohibiting the free exercise [of religion]' in violation of the Clause if it sought to ban the performance of (or abstention from) physical acts solely because of their religious motivation, the Clause does not relieve an individual of the obligation to comply with a law that incidentally forbids (or requires) the performance of an act that his religious belief requires (or forbids) if the law is not specifically directed to religious practice and is otherwise constitutional as applied to those who engage in the specified act for nonreligious reasons. (Ibid.)

Thus, when faced with the hard legal case generated by exceptionless legal norms jurists distinguish, as does DER in morality, between the intent of the law (and, sometimes, of legislators) and the effects of the law.

According to this line of reasoning, a law may not have the intent or purpose of restricting religion. Thus, a law the point of which was to require or forbid certain religious beliefs or conduct would be unconstitutional. However, a law that does not seek to restrict religion may have the effect of restricting religion, when it is an otherwise neutral, generally applicable law. A neutral law is one that does not in its very terms address religion. A generally applicable law is one that extends broadly beyond only religious activity. When a law is generally applicable it is understood to be neutral. A law, however, may be neutral and not generally applicable. For example, if religious structures had certain idiosyncratic architectural elements, laws extending solely to such architectural features could be neutral (that is, they need not refer to the structures as religious), yet not of general applicability (that is, not applying to non-religious structures). In logical terms, one might think of a law's neutrality as consisting in the non-religious intension or meaning of the words it employs. A law's general applicability consists in its having a broad extension (or reference) beyond religious activities. In *Smith* the majority held that neutral, generally applicable laws may have the effect of restricting religion. The majority determined that if a law were not neutral or were not generally applicable, then it would be unconstitutional unless it were both narrowly crafted to avoid restricting the free exercise of religion and justified by a compelling state interest.

While this opinion was not unanimous, all jurists did agree to the unconstitutionality of a law if its intent were to restrict religious belief or conduct. Moreover, they agreed in distinguishing the unconstitutional character of such laws from the possibly constitutional character of laws that have the effect of restricting religious belief or conduct while lacking such a constitutionally unacceptable intent.

Thus, jurists advocate a legal analogue to ethic's double-effect reasoning. For, as laws bear on those acts protected by absolute legal norms (such as religious conduct), jurists distinguish the intent of law from its effects. For example, a law that prohibits the possession of a certain type of material on which a religion transmitted its scriptures might be constitutional, while a law that targeted those beliefs insofar as they were religious would not in any circumstances be constitutional.

5.8.   DER AND ROMAN CATHOLIC MORAL THEOLOGY

As noted in Chapter 1, double effect originates in Aquinas's interpretation of Augustine's prohibition of a private individual's homicidal self-defence. Aquinas's inchoate account serves as the point of departure for the work of subsequent moral theologians, from St Antoninus of the fifteenth century to Gury of the nineteenth. From the influence of such thinkers, and because of its basis in sound thinking, double effect has come to inform law and policy. Given its origins in the work of venerable Catholic theologians such as Aquinas, one naturally finds it relied upon by the Roman Catholic Church in addressing relevant cases. This does not surprise; more interestingly, one finds official Roman Catholic documents employing DER. For example, in its condemnation of euthanasia, the *Catechism of the Catholic Church* says 'the use of painkillers to alleviate the sufferings of the dying, even at the risk of shortening their days, can be morally in conformity with human dignity if death is not willed as an end or a means, but only foreseen and tolerated as inevitable' (Catholic Church 1994, para. 2279, 549).

When referring to double effect, official Church documents often speak of 'direct' or 'indirect' acts. For example, the *Catechism* says, 'direct abortion, that is, abortion willed as an end or as a means, is . . . gravely contrary to the moral law' (ibid., para. 2322, 558). This condemnation contrasts with the acceptance of the hysterectomy case cited throughout this work (what might be called an 'indirect abortion').

Similarly, direct sterilization (for a contraceptive purpose) contrasts with indirect sterilization that accompanies the removal of, for example, cancerous testicles (ibid., para. 2399, 576). (As noted in section 3.1.2, there are reasons to prefer intended/foreseen to direct/indirect; for example, those who employ the latter terms typically define them using the former.)

A more extended official treatment of a case relying on double effect concerns terminal sedation. In October 1956 the Italian Society of Anaesthesiology asked Pope Pius XII: 'can narcotics be used even if the lessening of pain will probably be accompanied by a shortening of life?' In February 1957 Pius XII answered, stating:

> if, between the narcosis and the shortening of life, there exists no direct causal link, imposed either by the intention of the interested parties or by the nature of things (as would be the case if the suppression of the pain could be obtained only by the shortening of life), and if, on the contrary, the administration of narcotics produces two distinct effects, one, the relief of pain and the other, the shortening of life, then the action is lawful; however, it must be determined whether there is a reasonable proportion between these two effects and whether the advantages of the one effect compensate for the disadvantages of the other. (Pius XII 1957, 48)

Clearly, Pope Pius XII here relies upon DER. In May of 1980, in his condemnation of euthanasia, John Paul II refers to Pius XII's acceptance of terminal sedation, stating that it, 'retains its full force' (John Paul II 1980, 548).

Given its clear official acceptance, one understandably finds DER playing a role in the day-to-day workings of hospitals affiliated with the Roman Catholic Church. For example, echoing both Pius XII and John Paul II, the directives that govern practices in the many Roman Catholic Hospitals in the United States propose that 'medicines capable of alleviating or suppressing pain may be given to a dying person, even if this therapy may indirectly shorten the person's life so long as the intent is not to hasten death' (US Catholic Council of Bishops 2001, directive 61). Of course, as is clear in the arguments throughout this work, one need not subscribe to Catholic moral dogmas in order to accept DER. Nonetheless, the official moral dogma of the Roman Catholic Church certainly endorses and employs the work of philosophy that constitutes DER. Thus, DER represents an intriguing instance of a philosophical approach to hard ethical cases that the Church officially recognizes in its moral teaching. Of course, this is not to claim that it endorses the specific arguments here presented for DER; rather, it endorses the conclusions of those arguments.

Indeed, reliance upon DER does not appear to be limited to the Roman Catholic Church. For example, in a joint statement from the Church of England House of Bishops and the Roman Catholic Bishops' Conference of England and Wales, one finds the claim that 'it is both moral and legal ... for necessary pain relief to be given even if it is likely that death will be hastened as a result. But that is not murder or assisted suicide' (Anglican Communion News Service 2004). To note another instance, in its positional statement opposing euthanasia (that it defines in part as 'a deliberate act causing the intentional death of a person'), the Salvation Army states: 'Full palliative care should be available to those with a terminal illness. Optimal pain control and the overall comfort of the individual should be the primary goals, even though as a secondary effect this could marginally shorten life' (Salvation Army 2004).[5]

How ought one understand the relationship between DER and religious faith? Addressing a somewhat similar question, Aquinas calls strictly philosophical arguments for God's existence preambles to supernatural faith. He does so because while such arguments rest entirely upon grounds independent of religious faith, their conclusions partially overlap commitments of faith. For example, insofar as Christians believe that Jesus Christ is God they believe that there is a God. The belief that there is a God is a matter for philosophical argument; the belief that Christ is God is not. The former may be held by philosophical argument or by faith; the latter, only by faith. In this respect, the belief that there is a God is not, while the belief that Jesus is God is, strictly speaking, a matter of supernatural faith. Thus, as Thomas Aquinas uses the phrase, a preamble of faith is a truth implicated by faith yet able to be arrived at independently of faith. One may hold a preamble of faith without having faith. One who has faith, however, thereby has a commitment (at least an implicit one) to preambles of faith. (Although, as noted above in discussing the official moral dogma of the Roman Catholic Church and DER, he need not have a commitment to the specific philosophical

---

[5] This particular Positional Statement is taken from the Moral and Social Issues Council for the Salvation Army in New Zealand, Fiji, and Tonga Territory. Other Salvation Army councils make very similar positional statements.

arguments of which they are conclusions. Indeed, he may philosophically disagree with those very arguments the conclusions of which he holds by faith.)

Other preambles of the Christian faith would be, for example, the immortality of the individual human soul and the freedom of the human will. One might think of these (along with God's existence, a belief, of course, shared by Judaism and Islam) as certain ontological commitments that attend Christian faith. Moral positions also accompany Christian faith (and, of course, other faiths also); for example, the moral norm against homicide. To the extent to which ethical positions accompany faith, philosophical arguments defining homicide and establishing its wrongness, for example, can be regarded as preambles to faith. Could one consider DER itself a preamble? Clearly, it is not as immediately implicated in Christian religious belief as is God's existence, personal immortality, or the freedom of the will. Moreover, it relates to Christian faith insofar as it attends commitments to exceptionless norms. One might think of it as a derivative and remote preamble to faith. Derivative, as it accompanies one's acceptance of absolute moral norms. Remote, as it addresses a distant (albeit important) ramification of such norms, namely, hard cases that inextricably bind good and evil. In this manner, DER relates to strictly religious beliefs without itself being one.

In this chapter I have addressed the issue of reparations and argued for double effect's application to allowings and to the wrongful acts of other agents as they depend upon one's own otherwise good act. Moreover, I have indicated how international laws bearing on the conduct of war, the laws and public policies of individual countries, constitutional legal systems that incorporate exceptionless legal norms, and the official moral dogma of the Roman Catholic Church each employ DER. While DER has a narrow focus, it clearly enjoys a broad range.

In conclusion, DER has much to recommend it as an analysis of how one may both do good and avoid evil in those instances that initially appear to admit only of either doing good or avoiding evil. Because of its historical salience, its perennial ability to interest and focus thought, and the profound goods and evils at issue, this work's argument has centred about the norm concerning homicide. Of course, DER does not establish this or other norms; rather, it assumes them. Nonetheless, to the extent to which it plausibly deals with hard cases associated with exceptionless norms, it shows those norms themselves to be reasonable, and, thereby, argues for their acceptance. One who accepts such norms aspires to do good while avoiding evil. Employing DER, one can live in accordance with this aspiration, even when good and evil inextricably bind.

Bibliography

ALAN OF LILLE (1855). *De fide catholica*, in *Patrologia Latina*, ed. J. P. Migne, vol. 210 (Paris).

ALEXANDER OF HALES (1948). *Summa theologica* (Florence).

ALONSO, V. (1937). *Explicación del Derecho de Defensa según Santo Tomás de Aquino. Excerpta ex dissertatione. Pontificia Universitas Gregoriana*, 213–46.

Anglican Communion News Service (2004). *Bishops Oppose 'misguided and unnecessary' Euthanasia Bill.* http://www.anglican communion.org/acns/articles/38/75/acns3880.cfm.

ANSCOMBE, G. E. M. (1957*). Intention* (Ithaca, NY: Cornell University Press).

—— (1970). 'War and Murder', in R. Wasserstrom (ed.), *War and Morality* (Belmont, Calif.: Wadsworth).

—— (1981). 'Modern Moral Philosophy', in *Ethics, Religion and Politics: The Collected Philosophical Papers of G. E. M. Anscombe*, iii (Minneapolis: University of Minnesota Press), 26–42.

—— (1981). 'The Two Kinds of Error in Action', in *Ethics, Religion and Politics: The Collected Philosophical Papers of G. E. M. Anscombe*, vol. iii (Minneapolis: University of Minnesota Press), 3–9.

—— (1982). 'Action, Intention and "Double Effect" ', *Proceedings of the American Catholic Philosophical Association*, 56: 12–25.

ANTONINUS (1959). *Summa theologica*, vols. i–iv (Graz: Akademische Druck).

AQUINAS, T. (1891–9 edn.). *Opera Omnia Sancti Thomae Aquii-natis*, vols. vi–x (Rome: Typographia Polyglotta S. C. De Propaganda Fide).

ARISTOTLE (1985). *Nicomachean Ethics*, tr. T. Irwin (Indianapolis: Hackett).

AUSTEN, J. (1991). *Emma* (New York: Knopf).

BEABOUT, G. (1989). 'Morphine Use for Terminal Cancer Patients: An Application of the Principle of Double Effect', *Philosophy in Context*, 19: 49–58.

BEAUCHAMP, T. and CHILDRESS, J. (1994). *Principles of Biomedical Ethics* (New York: Oxford University Press).

BENNETT, J. (1966). 'Whatever the Consequences', *Analysis*, 26: 83–112.

—— (1995). *The Act Itself* (Oxford: Clarendon Press).

BOYLE, J. (1977). 'Double-effect and a Certain Type of Embryotomy', *Irish Theological Quarterly*, 44: 303–18.

—— (1978). 'Praeter Intentionem in Aquinas', *The Thomist*, 42: 649–65.

—— (1980). 'Toward Understanding the Principle of Double Effect', *Ethics*, 90: 527–38.

—— (1991). 'Who is Entitled to Double Effect?', *Journal of Medicine and Philosophy*, 16: 475–94.

BRATMAN, M. (1987). *Intention, Plans, and Practical Reason* (Cambridge, Mass.: Harvard University Press).

BYOCK, I. (1997). *Dying Well: Prospects for Growth at the End of Life* (New York: Riverhead Books).

CAJETAN, T. (1891–9). *Commentariis Prima et Secunda Secundae Summa Theologiae*, in *Opera Omnia Sancti Thomae Aquinatis*, vols. vi–x (Rome: Typographia Polyglotta S. C. De Propaganda Fide).

CASEY, J. (1971). 'Actions and Consequences', in id. (ed.), *Morality and Moral Reasoning* (London: Methuen), 155–205.

Catholic Church (1994). *Catechism of the Catholic Church* (Washington, DC: United States Catholic Conference).

CAVANAUGH, T. (1997). 'Aquinas's Account of Double Effect', *The Thomist*, 61: 107–21.

CONNELL, F. (1967). 'Principle of Double Effect', in *New Catholic Encyclopedia*, vol. iv (New York: McGraw-Hill), 1020–2.

COONEY, W. (1989). 'Affirmative Action and the Doctrine of Double Effect', *Journal of Applied Philosophy*, 16: 201–4.

COUGHLAN, M. (1990). 'Using People', *Bioethics*, 4: 55–61.

D'ARCY, E. (1963). *Human Acts* (Oxford: Clarendon Press).

DAVIS, H. (1946). *Moral and Pastoral Theology*, vol. i, 4th edn. (London: Longman).

DE LUGO, J. (1868–9). *Disputationes scholasticae et morales*, vols. i–viii (Paris: Vivès).

DEVINE, P. (1974). 'The Principle of Double Effect', *American Journal of Jurisprudence*, 19: 44–60.

DONAGAN, A. (1977). *The Theory of Morality* (Chicago: Chicago University Press).

—— (1985). 'Comments on Dan Brock and Terrence Reynolds', *Ethics*, 95: 874–86.

FINNIS, J. (1991). 'Intention and Side-Effects', in R. Frey and C. Morris (eds.), *Liability and Responsibility* (Cambridge: Cambridge University Press), 32–64.

—— BOYLE, J., and GRISEZ, G. (1987). *Nuclear Deterrence, Morality and Realism* (Oxford: Clarendon Press).

—— GRISEZ, G., and BOYLE, J. (2001). ' "Direct" and "Indirect": A Reply to Critics of Our Action Theory', *The Thomist*, 65: 1–44.

FISCHER, J., RAVIZZA, M., and COPP, D. (1993). 'Quinn on Double Effect: The Problem of "Closeness" ', *Ethics*, 103: 707–25.

FLANNERY, K. (2001). *Acts Amid Precepts* (Washington, DC: Catholic University of America Press).

Foot, P. (1978). 'The Problem of Abortion and the Doctrine of Double Effect', in *Virtues and Vices* (Berkeley: University of California Press), 19–32.

—— (1985). 'Morality, Action and Outcome', in T. Honderich (ed.), *Morality and Objectivity* (London: Routledge & Kegan Paul), 23–38.

Frankena, W. (1978). 'McCormick and the Traditional Distinction', in R. McCormick and P. Ramsey (eds.), *Doing Evil to Achieve Good: Moral Choice in Conflict Situations* (Chicago: Loyola University Press), 145–64.

—— (1980). *Thinking About Morality* (Ann Arbor, Mich.: University of Michigan Press).

Fried, C. (1978). *Right and Wrong* (Cambridge, Mass.: Harvard University Press).

Garcia, J. L. A. (1993). 'The New Critique of Anti-Consequentialist Moral Theory', *Philosophical Studies*, 1: 1–32.

Ghoos, J. (1951). 'L'Acte a double effet, étude de théologie positive', *Ephemerides Theologicae Lovanienses*, 27: 30–52.

Gury, J. (1874). *Compendium Theologiae Moralis* (Regensburg: Georgii Josephi Manz).

Hart, H. L. A. (1967). 'Intention and Punishment', *The Oxford Review*, 4: 5–22.

Hoose, B. (1987). *Proportionalism: The American Debate and its European Roots* (Washington, DC: Georgetown University Press).

John Paul II, Pope (1980). *Acta Apostolica Sedis*, 72 (Vatican City: Libreria Editrice Vaticana).

—— (1993). *Veritatis Splendor* (Boston: St Paul Books and Media).

Jonsen, A. and Toulmin, S. (1988). *The Abuse of Casuistry* (Berkeley: University of California Press).

KACZOR, C. (2002). *Proportionalism and the Natural Law Tradition* (Washington, DC: Catholic University Press).

KAMM, F. (1992). 'Non-consequentialism, the Person as End-in-Itself, and the Significance of Status', *Philosophy and Public Affairs*, 21: 354–89.

—— (1996). *Morality, Mortality: Rights, Duties, and Status*, vol. ii (New York: Oxford University Press).

KANT, I. (1998). *Groundwork of the Metaphysics of Morals*, tr. M. Gregor (Cambridge: Cambridge University Press).

KENNY, A. (1968). 'Intention and Purpose in Law', in R. S. Summers (ed.), *Essays in Legal Philosophy* (Berkeley: University of California Press), 146–63.

—— (1973). 'The History of Intention in Ethics', in *The Anatomy of the Soul: Historical Essays in the Philosophy of Mind* (Oxford: Basil Blackwell), 129–47.

KHATCHADOURIAN, H. (1988). 'Is the Principle of Double Effect Morally Acceptable?', *International Philosophical Quarterly*, 28: 21–30.

KNAUER, P. (1967a). 'The Hermeneutic Function of the Principle of Double Effect', *Natural Law Forum*, 12: 132–62.

—— (1967b). 'The Principle of the Double Effect', *Theology Digest*, 15: 100–5.

LEVY, S. (1986). 'The Principle of Double Effect', *The Journal of Value Inquiry*, 20: 29–40.

LIGUORI, A. (1954). *Opera Moralia*, vols. i–iv (Graz: Akademische Druck).

LYONS, E. (2005). '*In Incognito*—The Principle of Double Effect in American Constitutional Law', *Florida Law Review*, 57: 469–563.

MCCORMICK, R. (1973). *Ambiguity in Moral Choice* (Milwaukee: Marquette University Press).

McInerny, R. (1992). *Aquinas on Human Action: A Theory of Practice* (Washington, DC: Catholic University of America Press).

McMahan, J. (1994). 'Revising the Doctrine of Double Effect', *Journal of Applied Philosophy*, 11: 201–12.

Mangan, J. (1949). 'An Historical Analysis of the Principle of Double Effect', *Theological Studies*, 10: 41–61.

Marquis, D. (1978). 'Some Difficulties with Double Effect', *The Southwestern Journal of Philosophy*, 9: 27–34.

Matthews, G. (1999). 'Saint Thomas and the Principle of Double Effect', in S. MacDonald and E. Stump (eds.), *Aquinas's Moral Theory* (Ithaca, NY: Cornell University Press), 63–78.

Mill, J. (2001). *Utilitarianism* (Indianapolis: Hackett).

Moore, G. (1954). *Principia Ethica* (Cambridge: Cambridge University Press).

Nagel, T. (1979). *Mortal Questions* (New York: Cambridge University Press).

—— (1980). 'The Limits of Objectivity', in S. McMurrin (ed.), *The Tanner Lectures on Human Values* (Salt Lake City: University of Utah Press), 77–139.

—— (1986). *The View from Nowhere* (New York: Oxford University Press).

Oakley, J. and Cocking, D. (1994). 'Consequentialism, Moral Responsibility, and the Intention/Foresight Distinction', *Utilitas*, 6: 201–16.

Oderberg, D. (2000). *Moral Theory: A Non-consequentialist Approach* (Oxford: Blackwell).

O'Donnell, T. (1991). *Medicine and Christian Morality* (New York: Alba House).

Pascal, B. (1943). *Les Provinciales* (Paris: Éditions de Cluny).

Paton, H. (1965). *The Categorical Imperative: A Study in Kant's Moral Philosophy*, 5th edn. (London: Hutchinson).

PATON, H. (1966). *The Moral Law: Kant's Groundwork of the Metaphysic of Morals* (London: Hutchinson).

PIUS XII, POPE (1957). *Acta Apostolica Sedis*, 49 (Vatican City: Libreria Editrice Vaticana).

POINSOT, J. (John of St Thomas) (1885). *Cursus Theologicus*, vols. i–x (Paris: Vivès).

QUINN, W. (1989). 'Actions, Intentions, and Consequences: The Doctrine of Double Effect', *Philosophy and Public Affairs*, 18: 334–51.

RAMSEY, P. (1978). 'Incommensurability and Indeterminacy in Moral Choice', in R. McCormick and P. Ramsey (eds.), *Doing Evil to Achieve Good: Moral Choice in Conflict Situations* (Chicago: Loyola University Press), 69–144.

ROBERTS, A. and GUELFF, R. (eds.) (2000). *Documents on the Laws of War*, 3rd edn. (New York: Oxford University Press).

ROJAS, J. (1995). 'St. Thomas' Treatise on Self-Defense Revisited', *Recherches de Théologie Ancienne et Médiévale*, 62, Supplementa, 1, *Thomistica*, 89–123.

SALMANTICENSIS (1877). *Cursus Theologicus*, vols. i–xx. (Paris).

Salvation Army (2004). *Positional Statement on Euthanasia*. http://www.salvationarmy.org.nz/SITE_Default/SITE_about/positional_statements.asp.

SELLING, J. (1980). 'The Problem of Reinterpreting the Principle of Double Effect', *Louvain Studies*, 8: 47–62.

STERBA, J. (1992). 'Reconciling Pacifists and Just War Theorists', *Social Theory and Practice*, 18: 21–37.

SUAREZ, F. (1856). *Opera omnia*, vols. i–xxviii (Paris: Vivès).

SULLIVAN, D. (2000). 'The Doctrine of Double Effect and the Domain of Moral Responsibility', *The Thomist*, 64: 423–48.

UGORJI, L. (1985). *The Principle of Double Effect; A Critical Appraisal of its Traditional Understanding and its Modern Reinterpretation* (Frankfurt: Peter Lang).

US Catholic Conference of Bishops (2001). *Ethical and Religious Directives for Catholic Health Care Services*, 4th edn. (Washington, DC: USCCB).

VITORIA, F. (1997 edn). *Relection on Homicide & Commentary on Summa theologiae IIaIIae Q. 64*, tr. Doyle (Milwaukee: Marquette University Press).

WALSH, J. and MCQUEEN, M. (1993). 'The Morality of Induced Delivery of the Anencephalic Fetus Prior to Viability', *Kennedy Institute of Ethics Journal*, 3: 357–69.

WALZER, M. (1977). *Just and Unjust Wars* (New York: Basic Books).

WILLIAMS, J., PRITCHARD, J., MACDONALD, P., and GANT, N. (1985). *Williams Obstetrics* (Norwalk, Conn.: Appleton-Century-Crofts).

WINDASS, S. (1963). 'Double Think and Double Effect', *Blackfriars*, 44: 257–66.

Index